CW00823515

A LINE ON THE WATER

A LINE ON THE WATER

WRITTEN AND ILLUSTRATED
BY STEPHEN HARPER

CREEL

PUBLISHING

First published in Great Britain by
Creel Publishing, Norfolk.

© Stephen Harper 1991

British Library Cataloguing-in-Publication Data:
A catalogue record for this book is available from
the British Library.

ISBN 1 873944 01 2

Typeset by Harper Lapping, Hethersett, Norfolk.
Printed in Great Britain by the Bath Press.

For further copies of this book and other titles available,
contact Creel Publishing, 20 High Street,
Cawston, Norfolk NR10 4AA.

CONTENTS

FOREWORD

By John Bailey

I seem to read scores of angling books each year and just sometimes, from out of all the dross comes gold; an author who can write in depth, with sensitivity and with real feeling for his subject. Angling writers of the calibre of, say, Lord Grey, Hugh Falkus or Negley Farson are, though, pricelessly rare and I am not saying that Stephen Harper is yet up there with the giants. This book does show however that he is touched by elements of their magic.

Firstly, Stephen writes with absolute sincerity. There is not a false sentence in the book. Every statement rings true with nothing glib and nothing surmised, glossed over and passed on as fact.

Secondly, Stephen shares some of that blessed ability to relate deeply with nature, a gift that contributes greatly to the Falkus genius especially. Wolterton Lake, the River Thurne, the River Wensum, Towertree Pool and the rivers of southern India are beloved by Stephen as places of beauty and magic and not just as providers of large fish. If the angler who has eyes only for his personal record list is a pauper, then Stephen is a rich man for his ability to appreciate and convey the soul of such wonderful places.

Grey was a great angler, writer and one of our best foreign secretaries. Farson was a writer, angler, reporter, traveller and adventurer of unique talent. Falkus is a writer, angler, fighter pilot and film maker of genius. In idle moments he can also create quite lovely paintings. So to with Stephen. Not only has he been a pioneering angler for twenty years past with the ability to write about his encounters but he is also an artist of real ability as the illustrations of this handsome volume loudly testify.

A Line On The Water records an important period in angling history. Through the 1970s and early 1980s, Norfolk anglers were in the forefront of the specialist movement. John Wilson, Martyn Page, John Judge, Arthur Clarke, Pete Stacey, Stephen Harper himself and a host of other names were vitally responsible for helping push angling along its road of development. This book is the story of these men who had been brought up on Richard Walker and who took up the running when he and his generation slackened and dropped off. In many places you can sense the tingling excitement of new theories, new discoveries and new successes.

So, read on, learn and enjoy and I rather think that like me you will find this a very engaging book indeed. Certainly it is one that will be long remembered.

John Bailey
August 1991.

A Line On The Water is dedicated to
Sim, Laura, Oliver and Alexander.

There is more to life than catching fish.

What's hit is history. What's missed is mystery.
Old Norfolk angling saying.

PREFACE

I have kept an angling diary for over twenty years now and since that fateful day of June 16th, 1969, I have recorded, without exception, every fishing trip in possibly too much detail.

A Line on the Water has grown, rather than was planned, from some of the more interesting pages within these diaries and I have placed the stories I hope logically, in chronological order within their relative sections.

Over the years, I have received much good natured ridicule from my companions with my on-the-spot jottings and scribblings, but I am hooked now and as the seasons pass, it is a habit I am glad I cannot shake.

Winter evenings in front of an open fire, wind and rain at the window, I can enjoy reliving any session in the greatest detail, be it spring, summer, autumn or winter. I hope the reader will enjoy them also.

Invermay Cottage
Old Costessey, Norfolk
September 1991

ACKNOWLEDGEMENTS

My warmest thanks to John Bailey for honouring me with the foreword to *A Line on the Water* . I would also like to thank John and Martyn Page for their encouragement, advice and help. Without them, my task would have been decidedly more difficult.

Thanks are also due to my mother, Mrs. Freda Harper, for typing much of the original manuscript and also to my wonderful wife Sim for keying in the majority of the typesetting and for that final, vital proof-read.

I am also grateful to the following for the use of photographs. Dave and Gary Humphries, Brian Cannell, and Dave Plummer.

TENTATIVE CASTS

"Tigger took up the jar carefully and held
it close until his nose touched the cold glass.
There was another little fish inside. It was
different from the roach for it was a soft
gold colour marked with bars, both eyes like
swivelling jewels. They darted about
inside their glass prison with minute
quivering fins."

'BB'
The Whopper (1967)

TENTATIVE CASTS

The hardware shop boasted an extensive section devoted to fishing tackle that seemed to cater particularly for the youngest of anglers. Untold treasures, in the many shapes of brightly coloured floats, hung in profusion from a long pole suspended from the ceiling. Rods of all descriptions lined the walls whilst reels and other mysterious gadgets resided inside tall glass cabinets that served as the shop counter. A musty aroma of new nets hung in the air and huge, baleful eyed fish stared down from their bow-fronted prisons, proving that some lucky anglers did catch such big fish occasionally.

Jam jars and minnows, sixpenny nets and sticklebacks; all were forgotten now. This was an 'anglers' place, its aura and atmosphere almost overpowering, claiming another very young recruit long before rod or reel had ever been held.

The fair haired man with the small boy, bought a long garden cane for sixpence that uncharacteristicly tapered towards one end. A collection of other angling items were soon lined along the glass top of the counter; a spool of line, a shiney, square edged tin of split shot, three assorted floats and a packet of tiny hooks already tied to gut.

At home in the garage, coarse but skilfull hands transformed the garden cane. A short length of hosepipe formed the handle, slid over one end and taped into position. The small black centrepin was in turn taped midway along and rod rings, fashioned from the eyes of safety pins, were bound at intervals with one at the rod tip. The garden cane was no longer, now transformed into a true fishing rod of somewhat formidable power for an angler so young.

Anticipation was hard to contain and after several practice sessions in a waterless garden, the day of the first fishing trip arrived.

The beauty spot lived up to its name with ease. Almost cliff edged, the embankment was held together by the tangled roots of gigantic beech trees that dropped away steeply to the sweeping bends of the reed fringed river below.

The old fisherman looked up from his rod tip as the man and his son approached down the slope and along the bank. He bid them good day as they passed and watched them start to fish at a spot just before the 'S' bend straightened. The boy struggled with this new and demanding skill, his father always patient with every recurring mistake.

But the minnows were, as always, obliging. The old man was pleased to see and hear the pleasure that five small gudgeon could bring, falling to small pieces of breadpaste nipped from the large ball wrapped inside a damp, white handkerchief. He was not concerned that even a small boy had caught and he had not. He was after larger quarry.

The boy's float dived once again and this time he was connected to a weightier opponent, the cane rod even bending slightly. After a splashy tussle, his father managed to grab the line and pulled a sizeable fish protesting into the margins. He lifted it out with both hands and showed it to a wide-eyed, incredulous boy, the first roach he had ever seen. The old fisherman came over and helped weigh the fish with his scales. Three quarters of a pound and if he could catch such a fish this evening, then he would go home a happy man, he said.

It was obvious from the sparkle in the blue eyes of the young child that another brother of the angle had been born in those few short hours by the river beneath the beech trees and the old man was glad.

Many years have passed since that evening. The young boy is now a man with sons of his own but it is doubtful if he will ever take them to fish below the steep embankment. It is still a 'beauty spot' but there would be little point. All the minnows, gudgeon and roach have long since gone from the river there and they will have to look elsewhere for a fish to put a sparkle into young eyes.

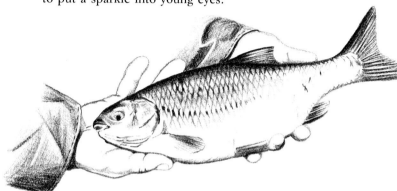

PART ONE

AN APPRENTICESHIP TO THE SPORT

"The passion for fishing usually begins in boyhood. I doubt whether there are very many who have taken it up late in life and become ardent enthusiasts, and later I shall describe my early apprenticeship to the sport."

MICHAEL TRAHERNE ('BB')
Be Quiet And Go A-Angling (1949)

Chapter One

A POND BY A MILL

T he pond could have been no more than half an acre in extent but it was almost one hundred feet deep and inhabited by large black and mysterious fish that lived deep in the thick, dark mud. Only on sultry summer evenings could these fish ever be tempted by an angler's bait, and then it was usually during a thunderstorm when all normal fishermen, especially young ones, would have long run for cover.

So began my long acquaintance with the pond and my introduction to still-water angling. Fatty Mallett had assured me that the information from his uncle was accurate and at eight years old, with only two years experience, who was I to argue, overawed by the silent, brooding water of such a magical place.

On hot summer days, during our over long, but much welcomed school holidays, we would head for the pond as if drawn by some unseen but irresistable magnet. The sleepy village of Drayton, nestling in the lush Wensum valley, would be left far behind as we pedalled our way up the steep hill, refusing to be beaten by the gradient until we reached the top

16

and could rest with honour.

A detour off the main road led us onto the woodland trail, under it's leafy canopy, sloping all the way down and we free-wheeled our bikes until the gradient decreased and then ended by the Low road. Furtively, we would cross the river at Broken Bridges, over the rickety and dangerous wooden framework that barely passed as a bridge, by Mr.Morton's tumbled-down, riverside cottage.

It was as if peering into another world, the clear waters of the Wensum, seen from directly above. An enormous aquarium and we scanned the sandy bars, between the gently waving streamer weed, for anything that moved. Roach, dace or gudgeon; even minnow. If it had fins and a tail, then we were interested but we never dared to fish there or even linger for any length of time. Mr.Morton did not take kindly to visitors on his bridge and was over-keen to keep his private road his own. He had even been known to set his dog onto potential poachers and as the years progressed, his character was to mellow very little.

And so we would hurry along the winding dirt track lane, through the tunnel of the railway embankment and beneath the rookery, where we tried never to look up, until, coming out into the sunshine once again, we arrived at the mill and it's pools. The pond lay only yards away in a field just off the road and adjacent to the river where it silently disappeared into the sluice gates only to come crashing out the other side, swirling, foaming white.

Almost surrounded by earthen mounds, obviously the spoil of it's digging, the pond only rarely became troubled by breeze or wind and our method to catch the small and suicidal rudd consisted of using a large bodied grayling float with maggots, bread paste or worm dangling only a rod rest's length below. The rudd would never take such a bulky float beneath the surface film. We would simply wait for the bobbing to begin, the ripples to spread and then strike.

Sometimes, usually when fishing a worm raided from a nearby tussock, a perch *would* completely submerge the float.

These instances were times of great excitement, the striped sergeant the prize of the day, usually being larger than our largest rudd.

I was content to fish for the rudd and perch for several years and must have been approaching my teens when, one morning, feeling rather pleased with myself, I had amassed quite a collection in my tiny keepnet. I felt especially pleased because sitting almost opposite on the far bank was a 'real' angler. It was obvious that he took his sport seriously. A self-casting reel and even a small landing net stood to attention, pushed into the reeds by his side. But he had caught nothing!

Perhaps it was his first visit I wondered, considering myself an expert having fished the pond for years. But he remained motionless, oblivious to my success, simply watching his red topped quill.

For some unknown reason, I decided to fish the 'Bullrush Bay'.

He couldn't possibly catch anything. What fish in it's right mind would pull down the wrong type of float? But something did and his heavy wooden rod took on a bend the like of which my rod had never seen. Much pulling and straining ensued, followed by splashing on the surface close to the reeds as he reached for his landing net.

From across the pond, it looked as if whatever filled the small landing net was large and black and my mind flashed back to those mysterious fish that dwelt in the mud. But it couldn't possibly be one of them. It wasn't anywhere near evening and we hadn't had a thunderstorm in months!

I rushed around to his swim, probably ensuring in my ignorance that he would catch no other fish that day and asked if I could see the huge creature that had fought so well. I expected a dark and ugly apparition, more eel-like than anything but as the folds of the landing net were parted, a beautiful and captivating sight met my eyes. It might have made two and a half pounds but to me it looked enormous. Shiney-smooth and warm to the touch with fine, translucent fins and a mass of tiny, delicate scales. Strong, olive flanks lightened to cream towards the underside and darkened along the back and head but nowhere the pure black of a mud dweller.

But it's most enchanting feature was the eye. Small but brilliantly red, it said much of the character of the fish. A species I would come to admire and respect greatly; a fish of summer dawns, of mist-shrouded lakes but rarely of thunderstorms.

To capture such a beauty was vastly beyond my meagre capabilities and I continued my 'bobbing' for the rudd until one sunny Sunday afternoon, lady luck took a hand in my destiny and forged forever the direction that my angling pursuits would follow. For some unknown reason, I had decided to fish a different swim today from my usual. An area not often frequented, at one corner of the 'Bullrush Bay'. Twice that afternoon my float bobbed and sunk completely and twice I thought perch the culprits. But not on this occasion. Two small tench had mistaken themselves for perch, had swum to close to the sun and met their downfall, surcumbing to my baited hook, suspended as usual, only two or three feet beneath the surface.

I had no landing net and had to be rescued on both occasions by another angler but from that day forth, the spell was complete, the die cast and tench played upon my thoughts and dreams to the exclusion of all else. The 'Bullrush' swim I occupied at every available moment for weeks that grew into months but eventually I had to concede defeat and acknowledge that my 'bobbing' was not the most successful of tench catching methods. There was more to this than met the eye and so I began to read avidly anything remotely connected with fishing and in particular, the tench.

Library books and the *Angling Times* , in the days when the Kingfisher logo headed it's front page, were read and re-read. Of particular help were a series of articles in *Angling Times* by the late Cyril Inwood proclaiming that to catch tench consistently you should 'Nail Your Bait to the Bottom'. My mistake had been revealed and from that point on, there was no looking back as tench began to regularly grace the new landing net that smelled so strongly of linseed oil. New friends were made at the pond and our merry band, Brian, Howie, Cope and myself caught many tench, the largest being almost half the record weight when John Salisbury's 9lb 1oz tench held that esteemed position. We discovered that the pond had no great depths but averaged between five and six feet. It was very popular with many anglers, young and old and eventually this would almost end the fishing at the pond.

Complaints about noise and an unsightly build-up of litter had almost persuaded the owner of the field, an elderly farmer named Mr.Phillipo, to stop the fishing. We took it upon ourselves to tidy the area and presented him with a proposition. We would lease the fishing rights, operate a day ticket system and keep it clean and tidy. So, for the princely sum of five pounds per year the fishing rights were ours and the farmer, a much happier man.

The arrangement worked well for several years and everyone seemed happy. The late Ken Smith wrote an article about our pond in the local paper but other storm clouds were brewing on the horizon and this time there was nothing anyone could do about them.

Apparently Mr.Phillipo had been approached by the local council who were interested in turning the field and it's pond into a small nature area, by compulsory purchase if need be. He was not impressed with this idea and decided that, rather than lose his field, he would fill in the pond. No amount of persuasion could convince him otherwise and while the land remained his, he could do with it as he wished.

The bulldozers moved in rapidly and began to push the mounds surrounding the pond back from where they had come. We mounted a rescue operation and many of the tench were saved and transferred to the nearby River Wensum. Sometimes they are seen during summer in the millpools and are even caught on occasion, probably giving the river angler quite a surprise.

As the pond gradually died, becoming smaller and smaller, we could no longer bare to watch and began to look further afield for our tench fishing. The remaining fish were eventually netted by the river board and probably helped to stock some other needy water in the area.

I have not returned to the field since those early days, preferring to remember the pond and it's happy times from the pages of my angling diary. The first rudd, the first perch, the first tench, even my first pike taken on a home-made spoon, all caught from the pond. It had been a very special place. A place where we had learnt the basics of angling, now just a memory and a vague and broken outline in another ordinary field.

But we can all dream and maybe, when I am older, with money to spare, I will buy that field and re-dig the pond exactly as it had been; plant bullrushes and stock it with rudd and perch. And what of those fish that used to be so dark and mysterious? They wouldn't be forgotten but I doubt that the young anglers of today would need to fish through thunderstorms to catch them.

Chapter Two

A NEW DOOR OPENS

O n days when the pond proved unreceptive to our endeavours, the millpools of the river lay only yards away and the dace, gudgeon and roach were always responsive. If we were extremely lucky, a grayling or trout would snaffle our trotted maggots, beating the hords of gudgeon and minnow, but it was quite rare and all the more treasured.

As youngsters we would fish off the bridges as all small boys do. The Wensum was a different river in those days with dace, gudgeon and roach abundant in all sizes. We had even seen roach approaching two pounds hoisted irreverently from the river up to the bridge, but most of the weightier fish would never make it and would fall back gratefully into the rushing waters of the weirpool.

Sadly, the roach have all but disappeared from the upper Wensum. Only a few old and battered warriors remain, spread out thinly between the millpools, the last remnants of once vast shoals. There are precious few small roach up and coming to replace them, the fry constantly wiped out by agricultural run-off or unable to hold their own against flood water, are flushed downstream as all the mill sluices are opened up with any outbreak of heavy rain.

Even gudgeon are not so common around the millpools at Costessey these days, although they still have strongholds in other parts of the Wensum. Dace are no longer as prolific and grayling are all but non-existent.

It was as this decline began that the chub, a much more robust and hardy species took advantage of the lack of competition to proliferate. It is an ill wind that blows no-one any good.

The chub were discovered to be catchable totally by accident. As very young anglers we would never eat the crusts on our sandwiches and they would enevitably end up floating downstream on the current. The dace were the first to benefit from our wasteful habit and it was not long before they were being caught, some quite large, on small pieces of crust fished below a cumbersome bubble float.

It was a real milestone that first day when the impressive bow-wave of a chub homed in onto the tiny crust. It disappeared in a noisy crash of water, the ripples spreading almost across the narrow river as I played and landed that first chub of around a pound and a half. A new door had opened to another part of my angling world. Like the tench, a worthy quarry that would always pull back hard, bend the rod and set the heart beating.

The surface of the river, well scattered with bread and crusts, revealed much about the chub population and it's whereabouts. In the beginning they could be caught almost under the rod tip if you were careful enough. As the seasons moved on they became increasingly more wary until we were trotting our well greased lines fifty or sixty yards downstream, waiting for that enevitable, splashy take and the long pumping back of the fish against the flow of weed and water.

The point at Costessey, where the two millstreams converge again, was always the best spot for floating a crust far down. It was as good as standing in midstream. You could guide the crust to left or right, which ever bank was favoured by the chub on the day. But just as it had travelled a fair distance and entering 'chub country', the enevitable coot would cluck it's way across river heading straight for your bait

*A worthy quarry that would always pull back hard, bend the rod and
set the heart beating.*

and the crust would have to be struck off, the procedure
started all over again.

I remember a hot, sunny Sunday afternoon many years
ago when the huge willow still overhung the river just below
the point, now long since felled. The bright, white speck,
reflecting in the sunlight had drifted and swirled it's way
downstream until it was lost in the distance and I watched for
a splash in the vague area where I guessed it to be. The coots
had missed this crust, probably fed to excess on my previous
offerings; but a chub would have to take soon before
the bait disappeared around the curve of the river where the
crash of a take could only be heard and not seen.

A smooth glide, adjacent to the distant, solitary
hawthorn bush by the right hand bank, was often a good place
for rising a chub. As the water crashed and the ripples spread,
I struck wildly and walked backwards through the reeds.
Certainly a weighty resistance there but it was possible the
line had sunk. It could be weed or fish or possibly both.

I had regained about half the line onto the old fixed spool reel and the vibrations detected through the rod reassured me I had caught more than just weed. But it became more difficult to regain line so I pulled harder and the harder I pulled, the harder it became. The reason soon became evident. Directly beneath the furthest branch of the large willow, almost in midstream, a chub began to emerge from the river like Excaliber from the lake. Not jumping or splashing but slowly vertical, it's head pointing to the heavens. I leaned the rod back hard and he shot up like a rocket! I slackened of and he fell back into the water. I laughed out loud but I doubted that the chub appreciated my humour and I made a concious effort to strike to the right on future chub fishing expeditions, thereby avoiding the trailing branches of that huge and majestic willow tree.

But it was a small price to pay for such beauty and the day they felled the willow it seemed as if the heart had been torn from that stretch of the river. Its familiar silhouette no longer broke through the mist at dawn, reduced to a pile of broken branches and regimented logs. We could see no reason for this vandalism although someone obviously thought it a hard days work well done.

From within those very branches that had hung directly over the river, Peter Hall and I once observed the largest chub that had ever lived in the Wensum; or so we confidently thought. Sprawled across those boughs, a leg dangling here, an arm pointing there, we had watched this leviathan from above for well over an hour. She knew we were there. That swivelling eye took in even the slightest of movements but was undisturbed. Old and wise, confident in her security she taunted us with her size whist we, in our naivety, fantasized about her capture.

We were inexperienced and to estimate a weight with any accuracy was impossible. But being only a few feet above, we could gauge the impressive length. When finally we climbed down from the willow, after this huge chub had tired of entertaining us and moved away to somewhere her presence would be less obvious, we each scraped a line in the earth well apart from each other, to a length we estimated the fish to be. After measuring these lines individually and writing down the results, the folded pieces of paper were exchanged and read silently to be followed by broad smiles on both sides. We had both written down twenty six inches! Even allowing for inexperienced exaggeration that fish was an incredibly impressive chub and I wonder if I have ever seen a longer or larger fish of that species.

Chapter Three

BAYWILLOW CARP
AND THE NIGHT OF
THE BIG CLOOP

There were larger things in heaven and earth than chub and tench. That I realised the day we discovered the carp lake and it left an indelible impression upon me.

We four teenagers followed them around the perimeter of the lake, through mud and brambles, in bewildered astonishment. Brian had lost his false tooth in the lake at his first encounter with a carp at close quarters; Howard thought they were pike but John and I knew better.

We had read our BB, Walker, Gibbinson and Keal, studied the photos and to us it was obvious that those purple, broad shouldered monsters were carp and we resolved to put at least one of them on the bank. Plans were laid, a prebaiting campaign embarked upon and sessions fished without success of any kind. Our confidence began to wane but not our enthusiasm. Then, when we least expected it, events took on a dramatic turn.

Our swim at Baywillow Lake was so overhung with willows, alders and brambles that it made casting almost impossible. There was just room for our small 'pup' tent and after casting out our crust balanced potatoes, we lit the stove and talked of mighty carp and battles that would be as dusk closed in upon us and the trees and shadows grew darker, then black. We each had a third rod set up that leaned against the brambles, rigged only with a large hook. If any carp were to be attracted to our broken loaf that lay scattered about the margins, then we would be ready.

John grew weary and retired to the tent. I volunteered for first watch and remained close to the rods willing the 'Herons' to screech into life and shatter the stillness of the lakeside.

The breeze that had ruffled the centre of the lake finally died and the creatures of the night continued their rustlings amongst the undergrowth. The mosquitos droned and attacked in the darkness until I too dozed.

For how long, I will never know, but it was certainly the carp that awoke me. It seemed as if every carp in the lake had discovered our floating bread and were attacking it with a determination I have not seen before or since. The air was full of 'cloops' and swirls. From under the very tips of the Mark IV's to several rod lengths out they moved. Swirling, clooping, bow-waving; searching for every morsel, however small or ridiculously large.

"What's all the commotion?"

John's muffled voice called from inside the tent. I was spellbound. He repeated the question and I replied with the highly improbable answer,

"Carp, bloody great carp, everywhere!"

They were feeding ravenously and it finally filtered through to my drowsy and disorientated mind that I must take advantage of the situation and bait up the third rod.

John was soon out of the tent and by now, much of the bread had been taken. We cast our baits out and watched the ripples spread and die, disrupting the reflection of an almost full moon on the mirror calm surface. A 'cloop', followed by a crash of water, close to John, reminded us that some carp were still very near by, their hunger as yet, not satisfied. We were so excited, it was a wonder those carp were not aware of the vibrations from two heavily beating hearts as we crouched so still and quiet in the reeded margins, watching that slowly moving surface, willing our baits to submerge, exploding the night into action.

The dark line traced a winding course to my crust silhouetted on the surface and a bow-wave approached, then faded. Activity had died down gradually and we feared our chances were slipping away. Then, almost on the stroke of midnight, one carp was finally fooled by the baited hook. There one second and sucked down the next. No 'cloop' or bow-wave, hardly a ripple and my line was snaking across the surface, disappearing down the black hole in the surface film where my crust had been.

I turned the reel handle, engaged the bail-arm and the carp's reaction was explosive. The rod was almost wrenched from my hands until I let go of the reel and let it spin wildly. But the carp was in total command. John crouched at my shoulder giving instructions and I tried to comply, but inexperienced as I was, I had little say in the matter. It kited hard to the left, under the trailing willow branches and finally into the dense and tangled web of brambles that grew downwards into the dark waters of the lake.

The line was slack and I reeled it in along with my hopes, for that night anyway. We looked at each other with blank expressions of emptiness that gradually grew into smiles in the darkness.

It had been a strange kind of success, one that had ended in failure, with a jumble of mixed emotions. The carp had left, the 'Big Cloop' was over, but we knew they would return another night. And so would we.

The season had progressed only a few weeks when, on the spur of the moment, John and I decided to fish a new swim, a bay at the south-west corner of the lake, where we had seen carp repeatedly show themselves.

This bay, along with other areas of the lake, we had baited with potatoes and that evening, taking sound advice from an article by Bill Keal, we threw out several more in a line across the entrance to the bay, hoping that any carp coming in would cross the line, feed along it and finally pick up one of our strategically placed baits.

It was Friday evening, very cold for late July and mist obscured the far bank into hazy shadows. The lake settled down after our arrival and we laid out the ground sheet, sipped hot black coffee and talked and waited.

We waited until 3.15am when my Heron alarm began to emit a strange, tortured whine. Damp must have seeped into the contacts but it had still done its job. I was soon out of the low chair and kneeling in the mud, watching the line hum and pour through the silver paper, vibrating at the butt ring and glowing red in the light from the Heron's buzzer box. It was my first conventional carp 'run' and I made the strike strictly 'by the book'. Picking up the rod, I extended my right arm and clicked in the bail arm. I waited for the fish to pull the line tight and then swept the rod back over my right shoulder and the carp was on. The instructions had worked!

Exactly half an hour later, I had him in the large, home-made carp net. It had been a battle full of anxious moments. In the pitch darkness I had crouched watching my rod arched against the dawn sky, trying to guess which way he would turn next. The carp had spent several minutes sulking under the branches of a twisted willow tree, it's trunk growing out half submerged, parallel to the water's surface. John had finally persuaded the carp to move out from this position after bombarding the area with potatoes from our dwindling bait supply. (I think he'd stolen the idea from BB and Dick Walker at Lackey's Leap.)

In the morning, as the sun broke through the trees on the far bank, gradually warming the mist off the glassy surface, I returned the fifteen pounder, my first carp, amidst gentle ripples and John snapped a very special photograph on my old instamatic camera. A picture that to this day, I have not bettered for its capture of the magic and atmosphere of how carp fishing used to be.

We had worked hard for our first carp, for that is how we regarded it, fishing together for a total of 170 hours. That fish could just as easily have picked up John's bait in the close confines of our shared swim and that is exactly what occured with the next carp we landed. We persevered on the lake although it was not an easy water, especially for two carp fishing novices. Many sessions passed uneventfully with perhaps only a tench or bream to break the monotony of an otherwise blank session. But finally, one of our baits was once again accepted by another of the lakes larger inhabitants and on this occassion, John was the fortunate captor. It had been lured by an exotic concoction for those distant days, Chappie dog meat paste, cast into yet another swim, in between the two we had contacted carp earlier.

The night on the point had passed almost uneventfully until dawn. Carp began to show themselves on the surface and

As the sun broke through the trees, I returned my first carp amidst gentle ripples.

we felt confident of a fish when John's floating crust bait was sucked clear from his hook. But before he could recast, his other indicator registered a fast run that could only be a carp. This time to the bottom bait, the dog meat paste.

In contrast to the swim where I had been successful, this swim was free of trailing branches and snags and John had only to counter the surges of the carp until it gradually began to tire and he could bring it closer and closer until it came within reach of the encompassing mesh of our huge net. In fact he had initially played it still sitting in his bed chair, so shocked at finally being connected to one of the lake's mythical monsters. It took John's brand new scales down to 22lbs 15ozs.

Those first memorable carp had meant a great deal to two aspiring but inexperienced anglers in those early days before boilies, optonics and 'off the shelf' carp angling. To christen our cane Mark IVs on such worthy fish was reward enough for those long hours of planning, hoping and dreaming. But when dreams come true, then any effort is worthwhile.

Chapter Four

ERIC, JOYCE AND STAN AT THE RAILWAY

As 'seasoned' carp anglers now, each with a big fish tucked under our belt, we began to search further afield for other waters worthy of our attention; waters hopefully not as difficult as Baywillow. And so we discovered the Railway Lake, but little did we realise that it would prove equally as hard a nut to crack.

The Railway Lake at Great Witchingham epitomises the secluded English carp pool. Situated within a nature reserve, a five bar gate cordons the dirt track that leads to the waterside and runs parallel to the lake, whilst trees and bushes completely cloak the lake's presence from all sides.

Today, the fishing rights are private but for many years prior to this arrangement, the London Anglers Association issued day and season tickets to their many members who would travel from far and wide to fish for the rudd and perch that over-populated the lake. It was these species that first attracted us to the water but once we discovered that leviathans pushed through the water lilies, the rudd and perch were soon forgotten and the lake took on a completely different mantle.

Long and narrow, the lake runs parallel and owes its origin to the railway line, hence its name. For the most part it is deep but towards the northern end, around the tiny island and bay, the lake shallows, the lily beds proliferate and it is here that the carp are most often observed.

Time distorts some memories but of those first sightings, they are quite vivid. Dark, impressive shapes sailing along the edge of the lily beds like men-o-war; broad, purple backs pushing aside the huge leaves with oily ripples, the yellow flowers on their long stems, twitching and swaying, then gradually still again as others, in their turn, also begin to move.

In those days, the lake was unusual for Norfolk in that it held any carp at all. There were perhaps twenty or so inhabiting the pool at that time but three in particular seemed to show more often than most.

Mike Saunt and I, (with thanks to Monty Python), named the smallest, a common of double figures, Stan. The middle sized fish, a mirror easily twenty pounds, we christened Joyce whilst the largest, an impressive leather closer to thirty pounds than twenty, we called Eric. His fame was to spread far and wide but it was Stan with whom we were to make first acquaintance.

Even as novices, it was plain to us that the carp at the Railway would be extremly difficult to extract from the lily pads although they did feel safer there and were more inclined to take a surface bait. In open water, it was rare to have carp show any interest in floating crust although they did cruise these areas often, if somewhat warily. But in the early season of 1971, the weed growth was to lend a hand. The hot summer had encouraged a thin film of blanket weed to cover the surface for a considerable area around the northern end of the lake. In amongst the holes, small and large, carp could often be seen. They loved to bask in the sunshine, secure beneath their canopy, a broad back here, a purple tail there and occasionally the sucking sound as a carp fed unseen beneath the weed.

John Judge and I had two takes in one memorable day in late July 1971. I fluffed my fish on the strike whilst JJ was

JJ was more skilfull. He met Stan at closer quarters.

more skilful. Fishing from the tiny island, he met Stan at close quarters, in the meshes of my landing net and recorded his weight at exactly twelve pounds.

Three seasons later, Mike Hill, another companion of our early fishing days, was to capture Joyce at 23½lbs, whilst fishing for tench with bread-flake and maggot cocktail. And only weeks later, during the same season, I was to have my first real encounter with one of the trio.

It was the 22nd of July, a Saturday afternoon and I started after lunch at 1.45pm fishing the lilies, after spotting Eric, Joyce and Stan cruising and occasionally showing interest in some of my free offerings of small, brown breadcrust pieces.

Sunny and hot, a light breeze rustled through the treetops but the lake's surface was calm, the surrounding trees shielding the water as always. I was using an Aitken Superflex blank, (a poker of a rod) and 17lb Platil Strong; a poor choice I now realise. The number 2 Goldstrike hook was baited with a piece of brown breadcrust about the size of a sixpence and I fished it half just touching the water, the other half just resting on the edge of a lily leaf.

The three carp continued to patrol the lilies and I concentrated hard on my hookbait, willing one of them, (hopefully Eric), to take it, trying hard not to dislodge it from the lily leaf as I held the rod uncomfortably, poking out through the branches that concealed me.

A carp approached, the pads stirred, twitched and the water swirled into tiny eddies around the crust as thick white lips approached, only inches from it now. The knot tightened in my stomach as I tried to control my nerves but it backed off and turned away at the very last moment and I recognised the light, pinky-brown of a leather between the gaps in the lily leaves. It was Eric and he circled back again and again, each time minutely inspecting the crust. Eventually even his acute caution was satisfied and his head once again neared the crust, closer and closer, the lips opening and all seemed in slow motion as the crust was literally sucked off the lily pad and was gone.

It was just before 3.30pm and a path opened up in the lily bed. The rod hooped over as if it were merely a light fly rod and the reel screamed out, shattering the silence, as Eric headed, in no uncertain terms, to my right, ploughing through the dense lilies as they swayed and the water crashed. I held on, keeping the rod high and praying that such heavy gear would stop this first mad rush. And then everything fell deadeningly slack. The water calmed quickly, the lilies gave a few final twitches and then everything was very still and quiet once more.

I thought the hook hold had given, I had held the fish too hard; but no. The 17lb line, now fluttering in the breeze, had parted as neatly as if cut by a scalpel, probably on a sharp lily stem. I retackled and desparately tried again, but it was pointless. The trio did not reappear and I packed my tackle despondently, not realising that that was to be my only encounter with Eric, although others proved to be more fortunate.

During the summer of 1977, the same year that I caught my first Wensum barbel, Ken Norton was to bank Eric and recorded his weight at 32½lbs. Later, he was also to be captured by Bill Florey, Rod Parnell and Dan Leary but many other highly skilled anglers were to be disappointed.

And Eric, (or should it have been Erica?), will not suffer the indignity of capture again. Sadly, he was found dead in 1986 and now resides inside a glass case, pride of place in the lounge of the Ratcatcher's Inn, Cawston, Norfolk; his long reign as undisputed King of the Railway Lake now finally at an end.

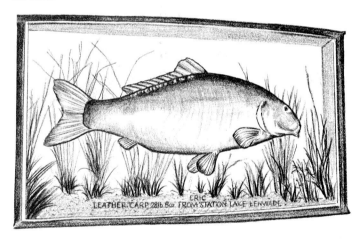

ERIC
LEATHER CARP 22lb 8oz FROM STATION LAKE LENWADE

PART TWO

I BECOME PREDATORY

"It was silhouetted, quite clearly, against a
clump of bright green weed that grew beneath
the water. The shape was unmistakable - the
dynamic, arrow-like form, the rakish dorsal fin
set right back to the tail for murderous
acceleration. But it was a miniature, a dwarf
pike, no more than a foot long. Even so, I was
excited. I tried to flick a worm in front of it,
but I was too near, the sun too bright, and it
flashed away into invisibility leaving a tiny,
dimpled swirl on the water."

CLIVE GAMMON
Hook, Line & Spinner (1959)

Chapter Five

APPRENTICE PIKE FISHER

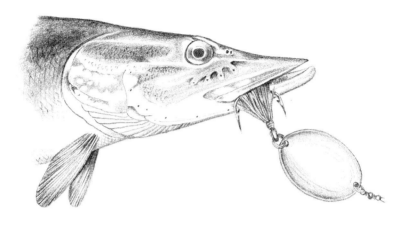

It was not only the summer months and their species that held our attentions. Even in the depths of winter, piscatorial interests received little respite from insatiable enthusiasm that began to show the first signs of obsession.

The memory of that first ever pike, taken from the pond by the mill, has not dimmed, although it was perhaps only a pound in weight and many years ago. The vivid greens and mottled creams, the pure white belly and the lean, mean aggressiveness, even in one so small. The needle-sharp teeth inside the tiny jaws that had clamped so securely onto my homemade spoon and red-wool tassled treble.

It had fired my imagination and I was in awe from this very first meeting; not with a specimen so small but with the history and folklore of its larger brethren, examples of which stared down from above many a Norfolk mantlepiece.

I knew instinctively from very early in my angling life that I could not ignore this famous part of Norfolk's angling heritage.

42

The lakes and pits surrounding Norwich were the first to receive attention and as they gradually shook of their summer foilage and slipped into the drab browns and greys of winter, only the hardy anglers, mainly the pikemen, would be seen on their banks.

In those early days, we were pleased with any pike. A seven pounder was big and anything over that size was just enormous. The ponds and gravel pits within cycling range were the first to be explored. Later, with the use of my trusty motor scooter, I travelled futher afield to sample other waters and eventually to fish the Broads for which Norfolk is so justly famous. With such a rich heritage and history of famous pike anglers, famous pike waters and most importantly, famous pike, it is little wonder that deep down, many true Norfolk anglers have a special affinity for the pike of Broadland.

One of the first waters I travelled to, a clay pit some fifteen miles north of Norwich near a village called Booton, harboured an interesting if somewhat grisly history. Apparently, many years earlier, a horse and cart had gone out of control nearby, missed the road's sharp bend and careered over the high embankment and into the pit, to be lost forever in the depths along with its lady driver. On certain nights, so the story went, the horses in distress could be heard from the waters of the lake. But I had no problems with horses over the years that I fished there. I don't think I even saw one in a neighbouring field, although I did wake up with a start one cold and foggy September night to find two large rats sitting on my feet. I think they were more shocked than I though, as I sent them into orbit.

Apart from its legend and its rats, the pit also had a reputation as a prolific pike water but without the history of big fish. A long thin triangle, it was almost totally surrounded by high banks and trees save for the short side that formed the dam. It readily gave up its jack pike but I never caught anything large there and I doubted that anyone else had.

Anything larger than seven pounds would have had trouble fitting into my small landing net, but on one cold November day, that was all to change.

My younger brother Nick and I had travelled through the freezing fog that morning on the motor scooter, numb with cold. It was a great relief to reach the pit and revive our frozen limbs. We squelched our way around the pit, through the mud to our chosen swim, the other bank barely visible in the fog. Here, we could usually catch a few small roach for livebait but we always took a few sprats, just in case.

On this morning however, I could only manage one roach and that was a little larger than I would have liked, but when the devil drives... I soon had him bobbing away merrily beneath the pike bung and I didn't have long to wait before a small jack had pulled it, with difficulty, below the surface. After feeling the weight of the fish, (or rather the lack of it) and setting the hooks, I handed the rod to an impatient little brother while I picked up the small landing net. Just as the small pike broke surface, amongst a flurry of spray, in a frenzied attempt to rid itself of the hooks, it was successful and one rather large livebait was now a rather large deadbait.

I cursed little brother for losing the pike but at least we still had the bait. After a brief pause, I cast it out into the fog once again as far as I could and began to slowly twitch it back. The first jerky retrieve through the swim and at one point I did feel some resistance but thought little of it. I finished the cast, reeled in and casting out again, repeated the procedure. The bait hit the water and sank slowly, eventually bobbing the float upright as it found its depth and I began to slowly twitch it back again towards the bank. I pulled the float,about a yard at a time,across the surface and pausing, lay the rod in its rest, flicking off the bail-arm just in case.

There is something special about pike fishing in a fog and even though we had lost a fish, I was enjoying the atmosphere of the session. I turned to see what mischief little brother was up to further along the bank and as my attentions returned to the float, I watched the livebait jerk the float, sending ripples across the almost calm surface. But I was sure the bait was dead! A pause, then the float was moving fast across the surface to my left, finally submerging and I grabbed for the rod, calling for little brother who was nowhere to be seen.

After a short while, I pulled home the two trebles with the Milbro eight foot rod and then something happened that I had not experienced before. The short rod almost took on the shape of a circle as I struggled against the pressure of the fish that tried hard to drag me off my feet, unprepared as I was for such resistance.

It was obvious that this was something special and in

45

blind panic I screamed out again and again for help. Eventually the squelch of feet in the mud behind assured me that Nick had arrived and I explained to him, in a shaking voice, what he must do when finally I managed to get this monster within netting range.

He stood intently with the net but each time I regained line, the fish would win it back, until finally the pike seemed to tire and began to wallow beneath the rod tip. At this point, Nick gained his first and only glance of the fish in the water and its vicious maw of teeth as it vainly tried to shake the bait and hooks clear. And he was impressed to say the least! So impressed at the size of the pike and its dental armoury that he dropped the net and retreated up the bank to a safe distance leaving me to shout at his heels and fend for myself.

Repeated pleas had little effect but I think I understood. To an eight year old it must have seemed like a meeting with the monster from the deeps. I would have to solve this problem alone. Luckily, by now the pike was played out and my small net engulfed her head. But that was all! Using the landing net, I pulled her in close with one hand and quickly dropping the rod, I grabbed her tail with the other and hoisted my prize ashore.

It looked massive. I had never seen a pike so large and Nick agreed, from a safe distance. A phone call to home ruined the Sunday lunch, the rest of the family soon by the waterside with camera and weighing scales.

And looking back, a nineteen pounder is still a very impressive pike but in those very early days of an apprentice pike fisher, it was stupendous, I walked on air for months!

Chapter Six

TIGER BY THE TAIL

In 1971, a book on pike and pike fishing took the angling world by storm. Fred Buller had written a classic and his labour of love, 'Pike', has since stood the test of time as an anthology of everything to do with our infamous freshwater predator.

As an embryonic pike angler, it became my bible and I could not, at that time, see how anyone could even consider writing another book on pike. I regarded it as the definitive work and even when the book was surpassed in later years by more up to date works, it still retained that something special that made it a milestone in angling literature.

There was much to excite within those pages, one story in particular gripped my imagination. It was the story of the loss of a gigantic pike by Buller on Loch Lomond whilst fishing the bays along the southern shore in the distinguished company of Dick Walker and Pete Thomas. Walker estimated the fish to be in excess of fifty pounds, having a clear view from his boat as it surfaced close by, "almost within gaffing range." Tragically, the fish was lost shortly after, coming adrift as the knot securing the trace failed.

I longed to fish those waters where the 'mossy-backs' lurked. Looking back, I was very inexperienced even to consider fishing a water such as Lomond, my largest pike still the nineteen pounder. But the lure was too great and when by chance, John Judge and I met up with members of the then famous Norfolk Grebes Specimen Group whilst fishing Ormesby Broad, the seed was sown.

Brian Cannell, Mike Saunt, Chris Gooch, Pete McLellan and Ray Brumhead had made the long trip from Norfolk twice before to fish the loch and had taken pike to over twenty pounds. They had met Ken Morris there on their first trip, a very opportune meeting as he had given them many useful pointers regarding the pike fishing around Balmaha.

We were invited to join their next party in the spring/early summer of 1972 and started early to prepare for our assault. Having been warned that heavy duty tackle was the order of the day, we equipped ourselves accordingly. Rods were, in the main, the 'Ken Latham', hollow glass 12ft. Dead Herring Rod. (I am still waiting to see someone using a live Herring.) With a test curve of 3½lbs, this rod was originally designed for wobbling herrings above the weedbeds on Hickling, Horsey and Heigham Sounds. Overpowered for this job, we found it an ideal rod for Lomond with its rocks, tough weed and even tougher pike.

An assortment of lighter rods completed the armoury, including lure and bait rods. The majority of reels used were multipliers. Ideal boat and loch-pike reels, loaded with lines from 12lbs for lure fishing, up to 20lbs for live and deadbaiting. Other tackle and gear accumulated over the weeks as our trip approached. Tents, stoves, camping gear, food, bed chairs, echo sounder, anchors and a multitude of other accessories, until by the middle of May, we were ready and eager to be started after the legendary Lomond pike.

As far as pike fishing is concerned, there is possibly no greater contrast than the broads of Norfolk and the lochs of Scotland. Norfolk, with its vast swaying reedbeds, silted and shallowing broads and monotonously flat landscape, broken only by the occasional windmill, has a special beauty all its own. The lochs of Scotland are at the other end of the spectrum. Their surrounding scenery is dramatically beautiful and anything but flat. To be afloat on Lomond during a spring dawn, the mist rising off the shallows and a flat calm, broken only by the occasional sea trout or salmon, must be experienced.

But Lomond is rarely calm for long and it is this other facet of its character that is of greater concern to the angler afloat on its turbulent waves.

These things I had yet to experience as our party left Norwich that Thursday night in late May. It had just began to rain; something we were to see a lot of in the fifteen days that lay ahead. Our party consisted of Brian Cannell, Ray Brumhead, Chris Gooch and Pete McLellan of the Norfolk Grebes, John Judge and myself. Huddled together in our Ford Transit, with every conceivable item of gear packed literally to the ceiling, we headed north. And the further we travelled, the harder it rained.

The hours seemed to drag by, the old van rarely bettering sixty miles per hour, but finally, as a dull dawn lightened the

Loch Lomond from the boatyard at Balmaha.

sky over Scotland, we enjoyed a breakfast of bacon and eggs somewhere on the outskirts of Glasgow.

As we neared Balmaha, we noticed the brooks that were normally mere trickles, now had swollen into raging torrents. We knew the loch would be high and coloured. Twelve hours and twenty minutes after setting out from Norwich, the roads and transport not so reliable in 1972, we reached MacFarlane's boatyard at Balmaha. Jimmie the boatman greeted us and as we had expected, the water was highly coloured and three feet above normal. The rain still poured down and a gale force wind whipped up 'white horses' across the loch's surface. Due

50

to the gale, Jimmie very kindly let us set up camp in one of the large boathouses. We discovered later, after a walk along the shoreline, that our intended campsite was three feet under water. .

After our walk, we unloaded, ate another substantial meal, set up our vast armoury of tackle and sorted out the boats. Everything was set; now all we needed was a break in the weather. The rain could be tolerated; the wind made it dangerous even to venture out onto the loch.

The next morning we were up at 4am to try a spot of lure fishing. It was still raining and overcast but the wind had died to a bearable 'light' gale. Not ideal lure fishing conditions, we returned fishless after only a few hours, the rest of the day we spent catching roach for use as livebait. We had come from Norwich with several gallons of maggots, but between six of us, and towards the end of May, they would not last long and we felt it important to build up a substantial store of livebaits as soon as possible.

The roach of the River Endrick were in pristine condition and everyone enjoyed wonderful sport, either ledgering or float fishing. Touch ledgering proved to be the most productive method, bites being bold and usually, hard to miss. We soon had our bait supply and too many eels.

At dawn on the following day, John Judge and I caught our first Lomond pike. All three boats fished 'the shelf' along the areas where the shallows drop off into the depths of the loch, our boat positioned between the other two. Our pike weighed fourteen and fifteen pounds and impressed us not only with their fighting prowess,(it was like holding onto a tiger by the tail), but also with their beautiful colours and athletic shape, in such contrast to our Norfolk pike.

On our return to camp, Ron Martin from Sheffield, whom we had met the previous day, told us of a 28¼ pounder and two smaller doubles he had caught the same morning. A very encouraging start and it looked as if we were in for some hectic sport.

Unfortunately the weather had deteriorated yet again the next day, the wind returning to its former strength and it was once again dangerous to venture out onto the loch. Only two of the group braved the elements but wisely fished from the bank. They were surprisingly rewarded with four fish including two doubles, topped by a 24¼lb fish caught by Pete McLellan. The larger fish was notably caught during a lull in the wild weather.

From then on the weather did begin to improve slightly, with the wind dropping occasionally and even some sunny periods between the rain. The fourth and fifth days passed by rather quietly, with several fish taken up to double figures, but much of the time we spent roach fishing. No real concentration of pike had been located so we decided that on the sixth day, we would cross the loch and try pastures new.

MacFarlane's Boatyard, Balmaha, Loch Lomond.

It was a long haul, (we actually rowed), but the weather, for now, was warm and sunny and the loch in the early morning had been mirror calm. In the shallower areas, down to about fifteen feet, every detail on the loch bed could be seen, including boulders the size of a small garden shed. It was quite an eerie experience, spying into the depths for the first time, but try as we may, we spotted no 'mossey-backs'.

We caught several fish that day, topped by one of 16lbs plus that fought for a timed eight minutes, even on such heavy tackle. The wind returned around lunch time and almost simultaneously, two of our floats were attacked by pike which left large gashes and the occasional tooth in them. We laced the area with a vast display of floating plugs, to no avail. These pike only seemed interested in our floats but by the time we had rigged them with trebles, inevitably the attention had stopped. It would have been really something to have caught a pike *on* a float!

Day seven was again spent after roach, the average size seemed to be around ½lb and fish of 1lb plus were not uncommon, the largest recorded at 1lb 7ozs. Previous years had proved breadflake to be a favourite bait. This year, all the roach seemed interested in were maggots, fished fine.

Day eight and we again decided to cross the loch. We started out, the weather overcast but strangely calm, one boat towing the other on the small seagull engine. Our boats were far from the nearest shore, the echo sounder reading over sixty feet, and then the wind began to increase. In only a matter of minutes it seemed, waves over three feet high were crashing over the bows, the other boat dipping and disappearing, then re-appearing on the swell of a huge, white crested wave. An adventure never to be forgotten by our intrepid band of Norfolk anglers. We were keen not to experience it again and were very glad to eventually reach the sheltering lee of an island. It usually took us half an hour to cross the loch. That morning it was well over an hour before we took shelter and began to fish half-heartedly.

A hair-raising experience for all concerned and we didn't cross back until the loch had quietened down quite considerably; even then we followed the shoreline fairly closely. Sport had not been too impressive either. Two good pike had been lost at the net and only one jack boated. The only notable fish of the day we found dead on a flooded island; a sea trout of perhaps 4-5 pounds.

Fortunately, the following day dawned less breezy and we again chanced a crossing of the loch after initially fishing closer to camp. It turned out to be a wise choice, in particular for Chris Gooch. We fished around the bays of the southern shore, scene of Buller's epic battle, with little success until around 6pm, when a wave from Chris' boat signalled success. The day had proved dour to our boat and we welcomed the excuse to up-anchor and witness Chris' triumph. And what triumph! As is often the case, a very slow day had resulted in only one run but the 'monster' had fed. The well worn saying,

Chris' magnificent 'twenty five'.

'It only takes one run', had been proven yet again; 25lbs 4ozs of battling Lomond lunker, Chris' first twenty, it proved to be the largest fish of the trip and fell to a drifted dead roach mounted on a single size 4/0 sea hook.

The westerly wind calmed gradually as we photographed and returned the 'twenty-five' until finally, the loch was as a mill-pool. We fished on into darkness, just in case there were any other monsters lurking in the vicinity but finally reeled in without further action at 10pm and headed back across the flat calm that reflected the surrounding hills and the setting sun.

After witnessing Chris' magnificent 'twenty five', we were all eager to return to the bay but it wasn't until after lunch on the following day that we finally anchored and cast our baits along the edge of the weedbed, our other rods covering the open water behind us. The westerly wind had again returned in force but at least the cloud cover was now broken intermittantly by brighter spells, the pike seeming to approve of the conditions. Glancing over to Chris' boat, I noticed that he was soon into a fish. Judging from the curve in the Latham rod, it was another heavyweight but unfortunatly the battle was brief, the hook-hold giving out, a despondent Chris gesturing his despair.

The next run came to one of my rods as a free swimming roach was taken and I pulled the hooks home into the pike which, after an aerobatic tussle, was soon moving closer to the boat. We could see the fish was sizeable and just as I began to get excited, the bait was ejected, the fish hanging just beneath the surface, dazed it seemed, by its experience. Nothing ventured, nothing gained, I quickly cast the bait back over the fish and slowly drew it back. Without hesitation, the hapless roach was retaken and the fight resumed, the pike making off very fast to the right, parallel with the bank and just beneath the surface, a bow-wave heading into the ripple. This time the hooks were secure and after another impressive display of walking on its tail, we netted an eighteen pounder after further problems with a flying treble that snagged the net before the fish was truely mine. A lucky flick of the net fortunatly alleviated this problem, the fish determined *not* to come aboard!

Most of the following day we spent trying to locate maggots around the tackle shops of Glasgow. Being a game orientated region, this proved to be not the easiest of quests but the effort was worthwhile. By dusk that evening, we had amassed a total of almost seventy sizeable roach and innumerable, ever present perch and eels. We were once again set for another day that turned out to be warm, calm and cloudy with initially very little wind.

As we rowed to our favoured areas, the black depths coming up sharply into the highly visible, rock strewn shallows, we passed amongst a vast shoal of powan that dimpled the surface of the calm, clear water for yards in all directions. Drifting so lazily, they seemed such easy prey and it was little wonder that the pike waxed so fat. We even tried to catch them in our landing nets but their lethargy was soon dispelled by this new danger as they dashed away into the vastness of the shoal that seemed to be heading around the islands and into the weeded bays.

Our livebaits seemed tireless for most of the day, continually submerging the floats and it seemed obvious that pike were close by but surprisingly, none were contacted until late that afternoon when a slight breeze from the east had developed and the predictable drizzle began to decend. The largest fish of the day, a sixteen pounder, had charged off on an initial run of over sixty yards, almost fouling the lines of my companions in the other boat before finally my tackle began to weigh heavily against its efforts and I was able to turn the fish, slowly regaining lost line.

Staying close to camp the following day, Brian Cannell and John Judge lost no time in boating five doubles to 18lbs 12ozs on wobbled deadbaits from the shallows. As we fared rather less successfully along the southern shore, with a ten pounder being the only fish of note, it was decided to spend what remained of the trip in a concerted effort in this area.

I awoke early the next morning, our last full day, and roused the others from their dreams of monster pike and home. The sky was clear, hardly a cloud in sight and the loch looked frozen, it was so still. Conditions looked good although our bait supply was very low but with what we had, we were soon fishing and into fish immediately. These fish were all jacks until 7.50am when Ray Brumhead, my boat partner, hit into something that decided to head directly out of the bay. 20lbs 10ozs ! Ray had another run at 9.50am but struck too soon. The only other double of 10lbs 8ozs was boated by Brian and JJ.

We all reeled in before noon and after lunch, again fished for the roach along the River Endrick to supplement our now non-existent bait supply. By late afternoon we were again piking, Pete McLellan ending the day very well with a 24¾ pounder, his second fish of the trip approaching 25lbs!

The last morning of our trip arrived and we were soon up and setting out from the jetty at 5am. Ray and I started in the mouth of the bay, the other two boats venturing closer into it. A north-westerly breeze brought cloud cover and a

Ray's fish decided to head directly out of the bay. 20lbs 10ozs!

promise of rain but on our last outing, it didn't seem to matter.

At 6.05am, I had a run that charged into the weed, the bait returning unharmed. But that was our only action, so at 6.45am, we also moved into the bay, Brian and JJ already having taken two small doubles. It was a wise move. We immediately contacted fish as I boated a very active 10½ pounder. Shortly after, another take developed into an incredible run that headed almost out of the bay as had Ray's 20.10 on the previous day. I began to think that I had finally hooked that elusive twenty pounder but could not be disappointed with such a hard fighting battler of 16lbs 9ozs.

Other fish continued to be taken as the morning wore on. Ray had an eight pounder, Chris a thirteen pounder and a jack, and Pete, one of 16lbs, but by late morning, it was time to pack up and prepare for the long trip home.

The holiday had flashed by it seemed. We had all done very well, seen lots of big pike, fished the legendary Loch Lomond and seen her in a variety of moods. I had seen five pike of over twenty pounds and one of thirty two pounds on the day we left but my first twenty pounder was not destined to come from Lomond as I had hoped, but from much closer to home.

Chapter Seven

A RANWORTH OPENING

During our eventful Lomond trip, I had witnessed the capture of six pike over twenty pounds and had yet to see a pike of comparable size from my home waters of Norfolk. A strange state of affairs for a native born Broadsman and a situation that I was keen to rectify. But then Broadland in the early seventies was in total contrast to Broadland of the sixties. The prymnesium wipe out of the Thurne system at that time not only decimated the pike population, it also ended an era of the great pikemen of Broadland who had made their reputations on those waters. It is of course true to say that pike were being caught on many other broads, in particular those of the Bure and Trinity systems but the work of exploration and rediscovery had, in the main, yet to be done.

In the early seventies, the original Norfolk Grebes Specimen Group, later to evolve into the Broadland Specimen Group, did much to pioneer a new era of pike fishing in Norfolk. An era I regard as between the two heydays of the Thurne system. The first heyday of the sixties, the second of the early eighties when, for a few brief seasons, a small area of the Thurne system returned to something of its former glory, producing more and even larger pike than it had ever done before.

But for now, the Thurne was not considered a viable proposition and our attentions were directed initially to the Trinity group of broads; Ormesby Broad (Eels Foot), Filby, Rollesby, Lily and Sportsman's Broad (Little Ormesby), and later to the River Bure at Wroxham and its ajoining broads.

The Trinity broads during the early seventies held a great number of pike, many of them doubles, with little attention from serious pike anglers. Sport was often fast and furious, large bags of pike not uncommon but twenty pounders were extremely rare, these pike reaching a ceiling weight of around eighteen pounds. During those early years, only one pike boated and authenticated by our close-knit group exceeded twenty pounds and then only by ounces. It was captured by Pete McLellan who measured its head at only a quarter of an inch shorter than that of the famed Endrick pike head, putting doubts into our sceptical minds that any realistic estimate could ever be gauged of a pike's size from its head alone.

Sport was often fast and furious on Filby.

It became obvious to us that if we were determined in our quest for Norfolk twenties, then we would have to search elsewhere. In years to come, the Trinity group pike would grow; first yielding low twenty pounders and eventually even several fish over twenty five pounds with rumours of rare, unauthenticated thirties. With these larger fish came the inevitable pressure of intense angling and its after effects. Pike with red flanks and split fins and it is now many seasons since I have fished there.

For now, we would have to forgo the action of Ormesby and Filby and explore new waters. I was therefore extremly interested when the name of another broad began to be mentioned in hushed tones. A broad where twenty pounders were not so rare. In fact Brian Cannell had taken his first twenty from there the previous season on a wobbled dead dace. Yes, Ranworth Inner certainly sounded a very interesting broad indeed and I was determined to see what it had to offer.

Unfortunatly, it only opened during the pike season for the last fourteen days and in that time, received quite a lot of attention from those anglers in the know. Anglers such as Frank Wright, Bill Giles and Reg Sandys, who rarely missed the opening day. A broad that could fire the imagination of these anglers, even after they had fished the Thurne system during its first heyday.

So, along with Ray Brumhead, Chris Gooch, Pete McLellan, Brian Cannell and Mike Saunt, we arranged to fish the opening day, Thursday, March 1st, 1973.

I had agreed to pick up Chris and Ray from Chris' house at 4.30am. Ray was late but we were still the first to arrive in my old Morris Traveller and after struggling along the path of sleepers to the jetty, we were soon loading the boats, the other half of our party arriving as we did so. By 6am we had poled our way out of the dyke and rowed ourselves onto the broad.

Ranworth Inner is a fairly large broad, greater in extent than its close neighbour Ranworth outer, known also as

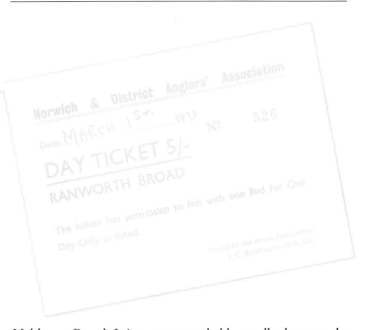

Malthouse Broad. It is not surrounded by reedbeds as are the Thurne broads but by a wilderness of dense trees, mainly alder and oak, so characteristic of these Bure broads. A large area at its furthest extent is reserved as a bird sanctuary and even for those last fourteen days is out of bounds to anglers. It is here were the sanctuary begins, that a large section of trees is inhabited by a colony of cormorants. Over the years these birds have turned the trees pure white with their guano, in the process killing the trees so that even at the height of summer they look bare, stark and cold.

In the winter months, there is no weed to worry about. The deep silt, that over the years has accumulated from the leaves of the surrounding trees, has formed an underwater desert, making any swim almost as good as the next, although the slightly deeper area around the centre of the broad did seem to be more favoured by the pike.

It was to here that we rowed in the half-light, a misty rain trying hard to dampen our enthusiasm in the overcast conditions. The wind for now was light, a ripple darkening

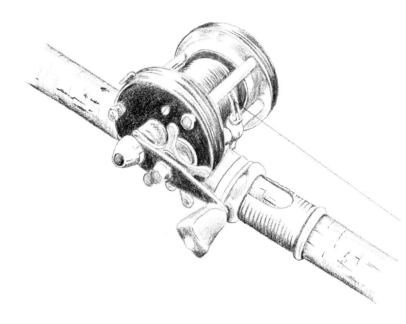

the surface as we positioned ourselves and secured the boats with the long mooring poles pushed deep into the silt. By 6.30am, the baits were out; livebaits and float ledgered herrings. The wait had begun.

Pete was the first to receive action after only fifteen minutes; a 13½ pounder. Later, other anglers began to arrive. We could hear their muffled voices from the jetty and the clunk and bang of poles, oars and tackle as their boats were loaded. Gradually, the white specks became larger as the boats drew nearer, finally mooring all around the central area and our three boats.

At 7.35am, Chris, fishing with Pete, had a take to an air-injected, float ledgered herring that after a short tussle resulted in his second twenty pounder at 21lbs 4ozs. After all those long weekends, often full days Saturday and Sunday on other waters without success and one of our party had taken a twenty on our first outing of the season to this water, almost within the hour!

By now other boats had encroached all around until the final tally amounted to fifteen. By the end of the day only four of those boats would take fish, three of them containing our party. And so our swim began to get somewhat crowded, casting even restricted in some directions and at 8.15am, Ray and I decided on a move further down the broad where we would have more space and cover unfished water.

As we moored up in our new swim, Ray drew my attention to Chris who was once again into a heavy fish, his Latham rod well round as a sizeable pike hung heavily near the surface. But within minutes, the action was over, Chris' rod springing straight as the pike regained its freedom. We learnt later that the single strand Alasticum wire had given out, multistrand wire in those days not so easy to obtain. Both Pete and Chris agreed that the fish could possibly have been Chris' second twenty of the morning.

From 10am, the action switched to the boat of Brian Cannell and Mike Saunt. Brian boated a 13 pounder whilst Mike had to wait another hour to net a 14 pounder and a small jack. These fish all fell to wobbled deadbaits; the 'Dynamic Duo's favourite method.

Finally, at 11.40am after we had introduced 'rubby-dubby' into our swim in the form of chopped up herrings, Ray had a run to a float ledgered herring - 6lbs 8ozs, a little disappointing!

The breeze of dawn had been gradually increasing as the morning wore on. Now at around noon, the cold northerly had grown to such an extent that our rear pole snapped leaving us with a swinging boat. It did nothing to help matters but we were not so easily deterred. With twenties showing up, we would stick it out until the bitter end, whatever the conditions. We just hoped and prayed that the other pole would hold!

1.45pm. I chatted to Ray as I slowly retrieved a wobbled dead dace. The tip shot round as the retrieve was stopped in its tracks. I quickly flipped open the bail arm and line ran out for a short while, then stopped. I felt for pressure but there was none, the bait having been dropped. The dace was very badly mangled, the teethmarks seemed large and I continued to wobble over the area for a long while but could not raise the fish again.

Lunchtime turned to afternoon and afternoon to evening. Other boats had had runs but no other pike of note were boated due either to dropped takes or fish coming adrift. It seemed the action was over, some boats having rowed back to the jetty. Then, at 4.20pm, one of my floats began to move upwind against the ripple.

The bait had been in position for over five hours, the 'rubby-dubby' put in over the session, finally taking effect. It was an air-injected herring, rigged with two barbless trebles, that was now on the move, the float sliding slowly across the surface, eventually submerging as I lost no time in setting the hooks.

I pumped the beautiful, heavy, solid resistance for a short while, willing the mooring pole to stay put, until the fish broke surface, over a yard of dark green and mottled cream and I began to take it very easy! Three or four times, line had to be given from the Mitchell multiplier. What a time for the star drag to pack up, the fish played out using 'button and thumb'. (Abu Ambassador 6000c's very soon replaced the Mitchells!)

"That's a twenty!" Ray confidently assured me after netting, the fish laid gently on the wet sacks in the well of the boat. The top treble lay neatly and securely in the scissors, the strike timed to perfection (with luck) as the herring lay across its jaws. The bottom treble, hanging clear, was cut free and the top hook then removed.

Weighed in a wet sack, the weight of the sack subtracted, my first twenty pound pike was recorded at 21lbs 11ozs. A day to remember. It was as I prepared to weigh the fish that my thumb slipped inside the gill cover and was badly sliced on the razor-like gill rakers. Only later did I realise how bad were the cuts in the excitement of the moment.

At 4.45pm now almost dark, our boats, first to arrive and

last to leave, headed for the shoreline at its nearest point to photograph the two twenties. Chris' fish at 39 inches long, girth 20½ inches, more on the stocky side compared to my twenty of 42 inches long, girth 21 inches.

In the torchlight, both fish were returned amid wet handshakes and swam off strongly. We rowed back to the jetty in the darkness and it was not long before we were celebrating our success over pints of ale in front of a roaring log fire with less fortunate pike staring down from over the mantlepiece of the 'Maltsters Inn'.

Two Ranworth twenties.

The twenties of Ranworth Broad lured us back after our opening day success but it was not to be repeated. Strangely, no other pike were taken from the broad during the remaining thirteen days. No angler, from the many boats that tried, even had a run.

Chapter Eight

A BOAT ON THE BURE

The boat was finally finished. Long cold winter evenings spent in the unheated garage, with frozen feet and numb hands had all been worthwhile. Even the water I used to mix the Cascamite glue was more often than not covered in a thin sheet of ice. But that was all forgotten now as I gave the boat a final coat of paint and made the finishing touches, ready for her maiden voyage on the River Wensum.

13th March, only two days of the season left and I launched 'Lucelocator' at Costessey Mill and drifted her a few hundred yards downstream to our chosen swim where we trotted breadflake for chub, or even a roach if one came along. Brian had the lion's share of seven chub that day (in fact he caught them all) and we packed up as the light began to fail, rowing the boat back against a strong flow to where we had launched the boat hours before. It had performed well and I was very pleased (at least it hadn't sunk) but now eager for the first pike trip which would really test her mettle on the following day.

Sunday, the last day of the season and I decided to take the boat to the River Bure at Wroxham. In the past, we had always hired our craft from the numerous boatyards in and around Wroxham but this was never an ideal situation. There was no way that you could fish on the spur of the moment; boats always had to be booked in advance, were often ill-equipped, dirty and with none of the built-in features that I had incorporated into my new craft.

Sim and I launched the boat just downstream from Wroxham bridge. She had brought a book to while away the hours whilst I put the boat through its paces. I particularly wanted to see how it would perform whilst float trolling, a method I had especially taken into account when kitting out the boat.

In the half-light of dawn, it was obvious that conditions were ideal; mild, overcast with little or no wind. By the time we had rowed the short distance to the area where I intended to start, it was almost fully light.

Two livebaits were rigged head uptrace and swung out, one into mid-river, the other to cover the margin. I rowed off, paying out line as I did so until at about thirty yards, I engaged the ratchets on the multipliers and began the troll at a slow walking pace.

With such ideal conditions, it was surprising that we had to wait for over an hour for the first sign of action. A take just downstream of the reeded section, always a reliable area for a run, and it was 'action stations'. The oars. with their retaining collars, could be totally disregarded; the anchor, hanging outside the boat, was simply released from its cleat, lowered and secured again and I was ready to strike almost immediately. At 4½lbs, not large by any means but a welcome start to the days sport.

Another take followed soon, this time to the midstream bait, but proved unproductive. We had watched the float briefly as it headed off downstream before submerging but the strike had not connected. Whenever I miss a run such as this, I always put it down to jacks. Wishful thinking on my part I know, but there is some truth in this surmise. It is more likely that a hookhold has not been gained with a smaller fish.

There sometimes seems to be more boats than water on the Bure.

Anything larger would probably have engulfed the bait and hooks totally at the first attempt, but it doesn't always work that way!

By now, we had reached the end of the stretch we call 'the street' and so I turned the boat around and headed slowly upstream towards Wroxham, keeping as close as possible to the bushes and trees that overhung the margin, the inside bait working the edge well and I felt confident of a take there.

The slow troll continued, time passed and the morning wore on. We had virtually retraced our steps through the swim with no other sign of action and so I began to consider the next stretch of river to try. The boat drifted slowly out of the 'hottest' area and I was about to reel in the baits. The left hand float hung close to the bank, a stark red marker against the drab surface, bobbing occasionally as the livebait worked beneath it. And then it was gone, only to reappear quickly and slip slowly and purposefully out into midstream. I silently hoped that this time the bait *had* been totally engulfed.

The boat had stopped and began to drift slowly downstream towards the float. I released the anchor cable from its cleat, lowered the anchor and secured it once again.

Reeling down, the strike connected solidly and I knew the fish was heavy this time. It came in towards the boat slowly and calmly at first, staying deep and I doubted it realised its dilemma, until it neared the waiting net.

Slowly but surely it edged toward me, gradually surfacing until only feet away, I had a clear view and could easily see the small bait hanging *outside* its jaws, one treble hook just inside the scissors. The net barely touched the pike, it shook its head violently, flaring gills and spraying water, the bait and hooks flying free. The long, dark shape paused for a second at the surface then sunk slowly, gave one flip of its tail and was gone leaving me to stare blankly at an empty piece of water and an empty net.

The livebait was totally unmarked and when returned to the bait bucket it swam around none the worse for its encounter and I wondered if the big pike had really been feeding, or simply annoyed by the small, silver fish that had the cheek to swim so enticingly close to its nose.

We fished on long into darkness as it was the last day of the season and took two more pike, the largest about 9lbs but they did little to compensate for the loss of the big chap. It would have been terrific to have christened the boat with a big pike on its first pike fishing outing but that was not to be. Still, there was always next season.

Summer, as always, had flown by. The long evenings had gradually shortened until it was no longer viable to fish after work. Mike Saunt and I had travelled to the Fens through the late summer and early autumn in search of zander. Now, as October passed its halfway mark, our thoughts turned to pike and the first trip in 'Lucelocator' on the Bure was planned for Saturday, 16th October.

It was a little early to fish at Wroxham. The cruisers would still be very active although not as intolerable as during the months of high summer when at times, there seems to be more boats than water. Not until November does traffic die down to become almost negligible in the depths of winter . At least the first two hours from dawn would be reasonably quiet and so we started at 7.05am at the Bure Court, a magnificent beamed and thatched pub that was later to burn down, leaving only its toilet as evidence of a past existence.

Cool, calm and overcast, the pike would surely feed today but after an inactive hour or so, we decided to move and rowed to the top of 'the street' where we began to float troll. I remembered painfully the last time I had fished this stretch and the loss of the big fish and wondered what today held in store.

Just after 8am, the first troll was begun, drifting downstream on the flow. Mike manned the rods whilst I controlled the boat, the two floats following about thirty yards behind, two bright red tops standing out like beacons against the drab khaki of the water's surface, until one sank slowly out of sight. Mike felt for the customary 'tap-tap' of a taking fish but it was not to be this time. The bait had snagged and we back-tracked to free it, recommencing the troll only to snag again almost immediately.

8.40am and the float to my rod again disappeared.

"Another snag!", Mike complained, as he tugged at it merrily, until the snag began to move off! We could see the float now as it left the edge and headed out into midstream. Mike reeled in his rod and I struck soon, the bait being only a small dace. She felt the hooks and began to fight erratically but heavily, swimming in towards us and trying for the now lowered anchor cable. Thwarted, she turned sharply and made for the roots of a large hawthorn bush, hanging out over the river to my immediate right. I side-strained heavily, first this way and then that, heading off each wild charge from these obstacles, the pike determined to snag my line around something. Finally, as she came slowly backwards towards the net, almost still now on the surface, I remember noting the incredible breadth of the head and back and knew I had hooked something exceptional.

Mike scoop-netted it expertly on the first attempt, closing the arms of the net around the bulk and lifting it

It was a little early to fish at Wroxham, we thought.

aboard. Laying on the deck it seemed to grow and Mike stated the obvious.

"Its a twenty!" I replied that it looked bigger than a twenty and after shaking hands and making too much noise, we up-anchored and rowed quickly to shore to weigh and photograph. 25lbs 11ozs, my biggest pike to date and at 43½ inches long with a girth of 21 inches, impressive all round.

The boat had certainly been christened in style this time. The first double to it and what a fish! A strange thought occured after I had returned the pike; I again remembered the lost lunker of the previous March and wondered how long my fish had been around this area. Could they have been one and the same? Had my hooks been inside those jaws once before? I shall never know for sure, but I have my suspicions.

PART THREE

THE LADY OF THE LAKE

*"The proportions of the tench, fins, head,
tail, and girth, are exquisite and well-balanced,
and there is something about the round
"deckle edges" to its fins and the thickness
of the tail-root which makes its appearance
most satisfying."*

'BB'
A Carp Water (Wood Pool) (1958)

Chapter Nine

WOLTERTON DISCOVERED

I first heard of Wolterton Park Lake in 1969 when a friend of the old days, Brian Bidewell, showed me a crumpled black and white snapshot of a young boy holding a very large tench that he claimed weighed over six pounds; this in the days when a five pounder was a dream fish. It was obviously full of spawn and carried the now characteristic 'football belly' but was still the largest tench I had heard of and seen confirmed locally.

He also had, pasted into his dog-eared scrapbook, a cutting of a feature from *Angling Times* by Ken Smith entitled 'Unstoppable Tench' that related to some exciting experiences with unseen monsters at the lake. Ken Smith, Peter Nesbitt, Brian and John Bidewell had fished the lake and caught many tench to just over five pounds but had been broken by larger, 'unstoppable' tench that had found sanctuary in the heavy weed that almost covered the lake completely, save for a few cleared swims.

Having no transport of my own at that time, it was impossible to fish the lake that lay many miles from my home, so it was several years before I was again reminded of the tench of Wolterton Lake.

I met Roger Nudd whilst chub fishing on the River Wensum at Drayton. We would often fish together and sometimes photograph each others captures. It was during one of these chub sessions that he told me of his almost unbelievable captures of tench from the lake including over fifty in one season during 1973, many over five pounds and most interestingly, two over six pounds, the largest at six pounds two ounces.

I had to convince my angling companion Brian Cannell of the authenticity of this report but the following close season we decided to plan a campaign after the tench, preceded by an extensive prebaiting campaign. At least twice a week, we made the long journey to the lake and raked and prebaited our chosen area, the boathouse swim, with mashed bread and swan mussels. We found during raking, only minimal weed compared to the days of the 'Unstoppable Tench' article when it had choked the lake in abundance.

As the 1974 season approached, we could hardly contain our excitement, longing to cast a line into the home of these huge, mythical tench that so far, we had only heard and dreamt about.

Chapter Ten

UNEXPECTED GOLD

S aturday, June 15th, we arrived at Wolterton Hall a little after 1pm. The mountain of gear for one all night session had to be seen to be believed. We loaded each other with bedchairs, rakes, buckets, stoves, saucepans, groundbait, not to mention tackle and bait and began the trek of about half a mile through the ornamental gardens and across the field. Here we acted as unwilling pied pipers to a herd of frisky young Jersey cows until we reached the first stile.

We hadn't travelled far across the field when a cry from Brian stopped me in my tracks. I looked around to see him flat on his back muttering something to the effect that "the haversack was a bit heavy". I shed my gear, glad of any excuse to stop and walked back to where he lay, pinned to the ground. With some help he managed to get back to a standing position once again but the strain was too much for the straps and the haversack remained where it was. The rather close proximity of a cow pat did nothing to help matters and we finally had to make three trips in the now scorching sun until we could collapse by our swim at round 3pm.

We slept as only the exhausted can until just after 7pm when we were disturbed by two local anglers on a circuit of the lake. It transpired that they too were down for the opening night and so, over mugs of hot tea we had a very long and interesting discussion spiced with more tales of tench to over six pounds, all taken apparently from this, our chosen swim. They told us that this would be the first time for several seasons that they had not fished this swim on opening night and we offered to move but they would not hear of it, wishing us luck and finally moving off, to set up further along the bank to our left. (Probably cursing us as they did so.)

The evening pressed on and, keyed up as we were, we soon had our tackle ready, swims baited and pitches prepared. Brian took the water temperature at 9.20pm, which read 69°F. Less than an hour later it had dropped by five degrees.

Our baits hit the water at the stroke of midnight as the hall clock chimned and we attached the silver paper indicators to the lines with trembling hands. We both fished two rods, one baited with mussel, the other with flake and not a word was spoken as we eagerly awaited what the night held in store. Fifty minutes had passed when the silver paper to my mussel rod twitched twice, then hit the rod as the line snaked off fast.

"That didn't take long", I thought and whispered to Brian, "We're in", as I struck, the rod curving over as a strong fish moved off fast in the darkness. But the vibrations down the line and through the rod were disturbing and I did not like to admit my fears. It couldn't be, after all the hard work prebaiting. It must be a tench! Brian's torchbeam illuminated the commotion on the surface and a long white belly reflected back, taunting us from the lake. The unfortunate eel, which weighed 1½lbs, paid for its audacity; it was retained and eaten later.

Still full of optimism we fished on. "They must be in the swim just waiting to come on the feed", reassured Brian and so we waited throughout the long, still night. Two months of prebaiting in that one swim must finally pay off and we tried all the tricks of the trade to induce the fickle tench to feed; to no avail. The perfect, misty, tench dawn came and went. Still no action. The other anglers around the lake had fared little better during the night but as the first rays of the sun hit the treeline on the opposite bank, Brian at last had a run to a

At 3lbs 3ozs, possibly the last rudd to come from Wolterton.

small piece of ledgered breadpaste cast well out into the lake, far beyond our baited area.

"No eel this time!" Brian exclaimed and he was correct; it was obvious from the struggles of the fish that it was no tench either. It did not take long to play the fish close in on tench tackle and as it passed through a small clump of soft weed, we gained our first glimpse, a flash of gold and red just below the surface in the gin-clear water.

I waded out into the shallows and netted Brian's magnificent prize and as I lay it down onto the dew covered grass, the golden flanks and bright red fins glowed in the early morning sunlight. We had heard tell of large rudd from the lake in the past, some even approaching three pounds, but nothing had prepared us for this unexpected encounter. Many years ago, large shoals of rudd and perch had inhabited the lake but as the years passed and the decline of the fishery set in, they had died off leaving only a few large fish with no competition to grow huge in their isolation.

At 3lbs 3ozs this was (and still is) one of the largest

authenticated true rudd from Norfolk in recent times. But there were no other signs of fish, whatever the species, for the rest of that particular session although we fished on until early afternoon. We photographed the rudd and returned it carefully to the lake, a fitting epilogue to the species at Wolterton, probably the last rudd to come from the lake.

The gear was packed and carefully dragged back to the car, another opening night over. A disappointment with regards to the tench and all our hard work but made totally worthwhile by that unexpected gold.

Chapter Eleven

CALM LAKES, MISTY DAWNS AND SWIRLING FISH

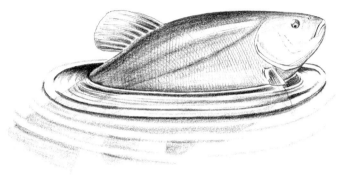

Taking into consideration the percentage of the National record, Brian's huge rudd was probably the largest fish ever to come from Wolterton Lake. But it was always the tench that attracted the majority of anglers to its picturesque banks.

A bonus fish in the shape of a large rudd or perch was always very welcome, but with so few left it made fishing for them alone an unprofitable exercise. We continued our campaign after the tench and gradually over the following weeks, we began to succeed using the tried and tested traditional methods of float fishing and light ledgering.

One session that epitomises this period of my traditional tench fishing readily springs to mind. It had begun as I headed the car slowly along the sweeping gravel drive of Lord Walpole's magnificent mansion. I remembered the owl on the gatepost and the rabbits, transfixed in the headlight's beam, darting away to left and right at the very last moment.

Turning the corner into the courtyard, I parked under the spreading branches of the chestnut trees. With the engine switched off and the lights out, the dawn returned to its silent, brooding blackness. As quietly as possible, hoping not to disturb his Lordship and servants, I unloaded the gear and arranged it about me as comfortably as possible for the long trek that lay ahead.

The door to the vegetable garden creaked and scraped on the gravel as I squeezed my way through with rod holdall, haversack and all. The gate to the tennis court was even more difficult to negotiate. I always managed to catch a net somewhere on the ornate metal leaves that covered it.

Once through the tennis courts, I plunged into the complete darkness as the gravel path followed its winding course beneath the canopy of large rhododendron bushes. A pidgeon, disturbed from its roost, startled me as it flapped noisily out of the branches and I walked on slightly faster until I reached the gate that opened onto the fields surrounding the lake. Keeping a wary look out for the vicious grey horse that had recently developed a taste for Barbours, I found my bearings from the familiar trees silhouetted against the increasing glow of dawn and headed out across the dew covered grass towards my chosen swim. One final fence, over the rickety stile and I could shed my burden and flop down hot and aching. It was still quite dark and the air seemed oppressivly warm and calm. Time for a cup of black coffee before the dawn caught up with me.

I mixed a small amount of groundbait, using the water from the lake that was still warm from the previous afternoon's sun. It was tossed a few rodlengths out to form a thin carpet over a small area. The chopped lobworms would contrast and stand out well. Several pieces of flake were also flicked out around and beyond the baited area along with a small amount of mashed bread. It almost seemed a crime to shatter the water's calm, to disturb this tranquillity, but it soon returned and as I gently slid the last rod rest into place, a silent swirl in my swim assured me that the tench were not far away. I noted the exact time in my diary, 3.12 am.

In anticipation, I quickly finished setting up and arranged my tackle tidily. I threaded a lobtail onto the first hook with a swan shot twelve inches away and made the first cast of the morning. By now the shapes about me had become more discernable as dawn reached its twilight stage. The tackle landed beyond the baited area and I gently pulled it back into position. The other rod, baited with flake, I positioned to the left just beyond the baited area and slowly turned the reel handles until the tiny quills sat up as small, dark markers on the silver surface.

I leaned back enjoying my peaceful surroundings as the light increased, changing the floats from black to a dull red. The swifts began to circle and skim through the surface mist and swirls appeared beyond my swim and I watched for the inevitable coot; but none appeared. I began to count the Canada geese as they filed past beyond my floats, heading towards the centre of the lake - 32 - 33 - 34 - thirty - float - no float! The 'flake' float lay flat and I struck wildly into nothingness. It could have been a line bite I reassured myself as I rebaited and recast. 4.22am and it was going to be a beautiful day.

The morning calm returned, as did my heart beat and my mind wandered back to the wildfowl. How could this lake support so many? I had previously counted 131 Canada geese, 24 swans and innumerable ducks, coots and moorhens during an unproductive session and wondered if this had any relevance to the inbalance of the lake that man and nature had created. The other species had suffered greatly over the years, the tench had thrived but I wondered how long this situation would last.

Concentrating on the floats once again, I looked from one to the other and as I did so, the float baited with lob tail twitched very slightly. I leaned forward, my hand hovering over the the butt. It bobbed again, dithered and lay flat, quivering in the surface film. I struck before I realised it. The float had not moved away but the rod curved over nevertheless as I guided the fish to the left, away from the other line and my baited swim. A female of 4lb 3ozs soon lay glistening on the grass, as warm to the touch as the lake's water. It was now 5.25am and a good start to the day.

After the swim had settled down, small patches of bubbles appeared along with tiny pieces of mashed bread. The floats often knocked or swayed as the tails of feeding tench moved the line or displaced the swan shot. 5.45am, I had just recast a fresh piece of flake. The float settled and went under immediately. Another tench very similar to the first but a few ounces heavier, soon lay in the landing net.

These fish had obviously disturbed the swim to some degree as it was not until the bells of the hall clock had struck seven times that activity around my floats returned, as did my anticipation. I flicked in several more hook bait samples to encourage the tench back and was just reaching for my flask when the line to the right hand rod tip tightened and I picked up the rod just before the handle started to spin.

I could feel the power of this fish was greater than that of the previous two as it headed out into the lake, towards the

As I waded out to return the tench, I was away on the other rod.

85

A big perch was always a possibility at Wolterton.

overgrown island and its roots and trailing branches. I had to give line on at least two occasions before I managed to turn the fish away from the snags and back towards the waiting net. It was an aching arm that lifted the mug of tea in celebration of 5lbs 8ozs of plump but powerful tench. I quietly waded into the warm, clear water to return the latest tench. I held her gently in the water glancing over to the other float just in case the impossible happened and inevitably it did! I released the tench and by the time I had reached the bank, the float was laying flat and slowly moving off. Grabbing the rod somewhere between reel and joint, I executed a motion that barely passed as a strike. But the tench had probably set the hook itself as it raced off to find sanctuary. As I played this tench, I wondered how many had returned to the swim only to be scared away once again by the frantic struggles of another comrade, but in time they too would be back. And at 5lbs 7ozs, I wasn't complaining.

Only one other definite bite followed that fish. It had resulted in a brief contact, the hook returning with its gape slightly widened and I had made a mental note to check them more carefully in future. As that session drew to a close with the sun hot on my back, it was almost midday. The mist had long disappeared as I began to tidy my gear and reflect on a memorable session.

Chapter Twelve

THE STORM BEFORE
THE CALM

Catching tench by traditional methods, using larger baits such as flake and lobworms, has always been very time consuming for often very little reward. It is probably due to the fact that tench never become pre-occupied to any great extent as they do with maggots and even boilies, baited in such great quantities as they are today.

When the swimfeeder began to make such an impact at Wolterton in the early 1970s, it took much of the magic from tench fishing but also changed it irrevocably, making the capture of many large tench seem almost easy. From catching one, two or even three tench on an exceptional day, the swimfeeder opened new doors. Great distances could easily be covered and areas fished efficiently where the tench felt relatively safe and free from the attentions of 'traditional' tench fishers. Six, seven, even a dozen tench could now be caught in a session. An unheard of success rate for those days.

But it was not all down to the swimfeeder alone. The phenomenal success of certain anglers at Wolterton was the result of a set of circumstances that occured at that time and peaked during the seasons '75, '76 and '77, when Wolterton was probably the best tench water in the country.

The lake at that time was populated by a large head of tench from 4lbs to over 7lbs and very little else, apart from the

88

occasional eel and a few remaining large rudd and perch. The lake was almost devoid of weed at this time, a rare occurance that meant that the new method could be fished efficiently, almost anywhere in the lake and the vast majority of fish hooked would be landed. The feeder was also being used by many very dedicated and knowledgable anglers determined to get as much as they could from the water and the method.

During '75 and '76, many tench were caught, mostly four and five pounders but with a few low six pounders. As the 1977 season dawned, the tench fishing was to peak with six pounders commonplace and sevens, at that time very exceptional fish, being caught there for the first time.

The following chapter chronicles the first week of the 1977 season; the storm before the calm for after that year, the weed gradually began to reappear and the tench became increasingly more difficult to tempt. It is possible that many of the tench, now old fish, had died off and not been replaced. It is also possible that they had become educated to the angler's methods and baits, but along with the return of the weed in abundance throughout the lake, they seemed much less in evidence and as the seasons passed, the tench of Wolterton became a very difficult proposition altogether. Some anglers persevered but large captures became unheard of and several tench in a session was once again exceptional. Today, sadly it is rare to catch a tench from Wolterton Park Lake, but it was not always so.

Opening week of the 1977 season; Martyn Page and I reached the lake at 9.30am on the 15th to set up base camp behind the beech trees on the east bank. The weather was atrocious. Gale force winds, driving rain and plummeting air and water temperatures. It didn't seem exactly conducive to tench fishing - or so we thought.

Joined later in the day by Mike Saunt, John Wilson, Terry Housego and Brian Cannell, we sat out the bad weather together huddled under the beech trees. No midnight start for us on this opening night. The wind howled, the rain lashed

Stephen Harper and Kevin Clifford with tench from Wolterton Lake.

down and I stayed in the bivvy all night, finally starting on the 16th at 4.40 am. By now the wind had dropped slightly but was still very strong and very cold. The clouds threatened more rain and my hopes were, to say the least, low.

It was because of the atrocious weather conditions and the fact that the wind was blowing down the length of the lake and onto the dam that I decided on a swim there. I assumed that until weather conditions improved, the tench would still be residing in or near their winter quarters; any that were not would probably follow the wind anyway. And so I set up pitch on one of the small concrete sluices where the lake's overflow made its noisy exit. Two 12ft fast taper tench rods were set up with fixed spool reels loaded with 6lb pre-stretched line. The terminal tackle involved a swimfeeder rig stopped by a small swivel and an 18 inch hooklink of 4lb line. These two rods were initially baited with four maggots on a size 12 Bronzespur hook but I later scaled down to a size 14 hook with one or two maggots. I used the two fast taper rods to fish at distance, for even at the dam, a shallow margin extended out bordering the deeper water.

90

A third rod, 11ft long and of softer action, was set up with 5lb line throughout. Again a feeder rig was employed but this time the size 8 hook was baited with a lob-tail and chopped lobworm put into the swimfeeder between groundbait plugs at either end. This rod I laid on the concrete, as I could find no other crevices to accommodate the third set of rod rests, and attached a small piece of weighted silver paper to the line to act as indicator. This rod covered the area of the slope where the shallow margin shelved off into the deepest part of the lake.

I had little to show for my efforts in braving the elements on the sixteenth. Only a hook with a widened gape and a lost fish. Mike Saunt fared better with five small tench, mostly male fish, to 4lbs 11ozs. Terry Housego landed a 6lbs 6ozs specimen and a new angler to Wolterton that year, Kevin Clifford, also landed a good tench an ounce larger; but it was an encouraging start. At least fish were coming out and I packed up at 10.40pm that evening after baiting the swim in readiness for the morning.

As the 17th dawned, still cold, windy and overcast, it was again Kevin Clifford that found early action, taking four six pounders to 6lbs 9½ozs. I had my first tench of the season at 5.20am - a 4lb male and John Wilson, fishing next to Kevin, shortly bettered Kevin's best by half an ounce. At 7.20am, the bobbin to my right hand rod, baited with four maggots, again twitched into life and sailed confidently up to the ring. I couldn't believe my eyes but soon had a bucking rod in my hands with the line singing in the wind. The fish felt decidedly weighty and so it proved to be at 6lbs 10ozs again and a personal best.

The tench just kept getting bigger and not long after, Mike Saunt netted a 6lbs 13½oz fish, at that time a new record for the Broadland Specimen Group and Wolterton Lake, but the lake record was destined to last only minutes! Kevin was soon into yet another big fish and after some problems with nearby sunken stakes, he netted another, a new lake record, 7lbs 6ozs, the first authenticated seven from the lake.

The activity was not yet over. I had no other action until 11am when a real humdinger of a bite crashed the bobbin into the ring. I managed to strike just before the reel handle started to backwind, 5lbs 14ozs - another good tench that had again taken maggots on the right hand rod fished at distance. Just over three hours later I had an exact repeat performance of the last fish, this time it weighed 6lbs 1oz. I fished on until 6pm but there was no further signs of life. It certainly was not fast and furious for me, with bites coming out of the blue sometimes hours apart, but the size of the fish when they did materialise, made them worth waiting for.

The next morning I somehow managed to oversleep and didn't get a bait out until 4.07am. Still, it seemed I wasn't missing much. All the other anglers around the lake were blanking. There were eight of us including Neville Fickling who had arrived the previous afternoon. The weather, if anything, had deteriorated. It was so cold I could see my breath and sitting facing the wind was no fun. I was wearing more clothes for tench fishing than I would normally wear in winter for pike fishing on the Broads and I packed up biteless at 2pm.

The next session started just as slowly. Pete Stacey arrived at dawn and set up pitch to my left on the dam. Most of the other anglers remained camped along the east bank, huddled in their bivvies or under brollies, out of the full force of wind and intermittant showers.

I had been fishing almost three hours before any sign of life showed on the bobbins. At 7am, much to my surprise, I had a drop-back bite that I hit too late and the maggots returned completely sucked. The only other bites seemed to be minute twitches that I tried striking at but could not connect with. Considering the conditions, I decided to scale down to size 14 hooks and just one or two maggots only. The tench, after their busy feeding of the 17th, now seemed decidedly finicky as I experienced another inconclusive run.

8.25am and the silver paper to the soft action rod baited with lobtail, slid across the concrete. I struck but there was no reassuring thump. The bait was still intact and I surmised that perhaps a fish had swum into the line. It wasn't until just before 10am that John Wilson took the first tench of the day at 5lbs 14ozs and that after two abortive runs to lobworm but it did herald a spasmodic feeding spell at last.

At 10am I finally connected with something that decided to put as much distance as possible between itself and me. The rod strained and I let the reel handle spin wildly as line was taken rapidly from the spool. I managed to slow the fish and it kited to my left. It made two other long runs and fought extremely hard close in before I was able to slide it over the net. The other fish had fought hard but nowhere as doggedly as this fish; I knew it must be an exceptional tench and at 7lbs 4ozs, it was! I was overjoyed. My first 7lb tench; a fish that dreams are made of. I decided to take some photographs immediately so I could return the fish but was interrupted by the reel handle of the single maggot rod. Another tench of 5lbs 14ozs. Martyn later took another, at an ounce lighter.

Settled down again, I decided to write up the session in my notebook but was once again interrupted, this time by the

The first 7lb tench; a fish that dreams are made of.

93

silver paper of the lob-tail as it slid across the concrete - 6lbs 8ozs. I pinched myself - it hurt; no I wasn't dreaming but for now the tench had gone off the feed although I fished on until the afternoon.

The next morning dawned the calmest so far. The wind continued to blow toward me, still cold but at least not as fiercely. I started the session in great anticipation and was not to be disappointed. Two more sixes at 6lbs 4½ozs and 6lbs exactly. The latter fish fought extremely hard; I just could not get it to the net. They both took single maggots at long range on size 14 hooks bearing out my theory that maggots were gradually being associated with danger. Martyn also enjoyed the session with two tench to 6lbs 7ozs.

The following morning was in complete contrast. So slow as to be stationary although Martyn later took fish of 5lbs 13ozs and 6lbs 5ozs. At 10.55am I struck a tiny twitch again to single maggot and was very surprised to be attached to something that felt like a very heavy tench indeed. I pumped it back toward me and was beginning to think that I had really cracked it this time when a twig broke surface, followed by a heavy swirl. I had them both under the rod tip and could see a small male tench attached to a much larger branch. It was thrashing wildly and finally broke free. Pausing for a few moments to regain its composure, it then shot off across the shallows, heading for the deeper water and leaving me well and truly attached to a specimen sized snag.

The last day of our short tenching holiday arrived. The wind had finally dropped and the clouds were tinged with white rather than grey. A small area of the lake's surface towards its centre, was rippled by a light breeze. The rest of the lake was mirror calm. It was still quite cold but later during the session, the clouds broke up and the sun finally made a welcome appearance.

We started at 3.25am and after only twenty minutes I had an uncertain bite to a maggot baited rod. Up - up - up - down - up - no contact. 3.55am and this time a confident bite to the lobtail rod - again no contact! Considering the average size of the tench being caught, these missed bites were very worrying. I consoled myself in the thought that they were probably lines bites, the baits often returning intact.

It wasn't until 5.25am that the next bite materialised. The silver paper to the lobtail rod twitched once and slowly moved across the concrete. I picked up the rod and waited for the line to tighten. The stike connected this time and the fish headed out taking line immediately. My thoughts flashed back to the 7lbs 4ozs tench taken earlier and I decided to take it very easy until I had that fish well and truly netted. She kited to left and then to right. I regained line, she took it. This seemed to go on for several minutes but the hook hold was secure and I was soon admiring an enormous tench on the grass in the folds of the net.

The hook hold was secure and I was soon admiring an enormous tench, 7lbs 10½ozs.

Dave Humphries was possibly the last angler to land a large tench at Wolterton; this 7lbs 12oz fish in 1988.

I carefully put the fish into a wet weighing bag and hoisted it onto my 8lb Salter scales and with a thump it took them to the limit. I borrowed John Wilson's Avon scales and subtracting the weight of the bag, recorded the tench at 7lbs 10½ozs. A lake record and the largest tench from Norfolk at that time.

John also had a rewarding session capturing his first seven pounder at 7lbs ½oz fishing to my left. Other tench of 5lbs 15ozs and 6lbs 3ozs fell to my rod later in the session and a 5lbs 15oz for Martyn but after the sevens they seemed almost small and I struggled to keep my fishing values in perspective.

Towards midday, the sun finally broke through and the layers of clothing were peeled off gradually as temperatures rose and the sun blazed down; but I wondered if things would have turned out differently had that been the case at the beginning of the week.

A Wensum barbel.

A chub swim on the Wensum.

Portrait of a Lomond 'tiger'.

A weight of 32lbs 9ozs was recorded.

Thurne pike. Our determination to succeed had paid off.

The Thurne system and an unusually calm dawn.

Towertree Pool was simply quite beautiful.

A Boat on the Bure.

I recorded the impressive mirror at 30lbs 11ozs.

Kevin Maxfield with a large Wensum barbel; 11lbs 8ozs.

A piker's sunrise.

The mighty Barbus Tor Mussulah.

From the top of the hill, we followed the sparkling green river.

104 pounds of gigantic, hump-backed, 'golden' mahseer.

PART FOUR

PATHS TO THE RIVER

"*The reel screamed with its tight clutch setting
as line ran out to the pull of this great force, my
fingers clamped down on the reel until
rod and line could take no more, but still the
fish did not turn. Out in the fast water,
the barbel turned downstream and streaked
in the current.*"

PETER WHEAT (Contributor)
Catch A Big Fish (1967)

Chapter Thirteen

BARBEL;
A FIRST ENCOUNTER

After such a successful opening week at Wolterton, I found it difficult to tear myself away from the tench fishing but I knew it would be unlikely that I could better the results already achieved.

Big tench were still coming out; Martyn Page took three seven pounders in one day, probably the first angler ever to do so. But I had decided to direct my attentions elsewhere, with very little idea where they would lead until one day, whilst on a chubbing expedition with Mike Saunt, we inadvertantly stumbled upon a piscatorial goldmine.

We had known of Wensum barbel since their main introduction in the summer of 1972 and had seen the odd fish now and then, but it was not until this particular day that we located what for us was a large shoal of about seven fish.

To our inexperienced eyes, the shoal seemed to range between 3lbs and 9lbs but the swim they inhabited posed several problems. The main areas they frequented were just out from the branches of an overhanging tree in shallow, crystal clear water, above sand and gravel bars alternating with thick beds of streamer weed. They were accompanied by a large shoal of over thirty chub in the two to four pound range and one solitary roach that was well over two pounds.

From the obvious vantage point within the branches of the overhanging tree, we watched our quarry and a plan began to form. The opposite bank was private but offered few advantages in any case. The swim could not be fished efficiently from our own bank due to the dense undergrowth, bushes and tree branches that would hinder casting. The only answer seemed to be to fish from the tree itself and hopefully subdue a hooked barbel with heavy pressure from above.

I suggested the plan to Mike and after initial doubts we decided to give it a try. One major advantage was the fact that a bait could be seen and placed in relation to a particular fish. Working as a team taking turns, one man up the tree and one at its base with the landing net, seemed a simply enough plan but there was one thing we had to find out. Would they accept our baits? We had a fair selection with us and tried a few samples, managing to drop them just upstream of the barbel. We watched in anticipation as they trundled along the bottom, carried by the fairly fast current towards the fish. Considering the fact that they had been rarely fished for and caught in the past, less than six landed to our knowledge, we were surprised at their wariness to our offerings. As our samples drifted down on the current, the fish would either move to one side or rise from the bottom to avoid them, if the ravenous hordes of chub didn't get there first!

Thinking a worm might do the trick, I broke one into smallish pieces and tossed them upstream. This time a small barbel mouthed a piece and blew it out. That, we thought, was a good enough sign and tossed a coin to see who would have first crack at them. Mike won and returned up the tree armed with an all-through 12ft carp rod, eight pound line and a link ledger. I waited patiently at the base of the tree slightly downstream in a gap in the dense undergrowth. I did not have long to wait. A running commentary from Mike kept me informed of how things were going. He had to pull his bait from the mouths of several chub before a barbel managed to approach it. I told him that he should pull it away from the smaller barbel too, but his will-power wouldn't hold and he was soon fast into a medium sized fish of around five pounds.

"I'm into one!" he shouted excitedly. "Get the net in!"

He played the fish for a short while but it could do little against heavy tackle and pressure from above. It was at this stage that Mike said he thought the fish was either foul-hooked or the line had caught around a fin. We never found out. I had just waded out thigh deep, (wearing plimsoles) when a very despondent voice from above informed me that the fish was off. It seemed as though the line had parted, possibly cut thought Mike, on the dorsal fin.

The shoal had scattered due to the commotion of the lost fish and so my turn would have to wait until another day. We spent the rest of the session taking several out of condition chub on floating crust and slowly sinking flake. Mike had the largest at 4lbs 7ozs, a consolation prize for the loss of the 'whiskers', but my heart wasn't in it. I just had to have one of 'them'.

The next morning I had planned a carp session as Mike was at work and arrived at the lake just after dawn. I had been enjoying some great sport there, fishing before work from first light to about 7.45am. Only rarely on these occasions did I not have the lake to myself, but being a Saturday morning and having arrived slightly later that usual, I found all the productive swims occupied and so decided to fish the other side of the lake. Several fruitless hours passed. The indicators had not even twitched and it was obvious that a blank was on the cards. I decided to try for the barbel.

I reached the river and by now the skies had clouded over and a fine drizzle began to fall. I didn't mind. I thought perhaps the barbel would be more inclined to feed in the overcast conditions in such clear, shallow water.

I parked the car and hurried to the swim, optimism seemingly making my legs walk faster. As I approached the swim of yesterday, everything seemed deathly quiet. No breeze, no sound of bird or insect and the drizzle continued to fall just as silently. I crept as quietly as possible the last few yards and soon found myself nestled in the branches of the tree. Slipping on my polaroids, I gently parted the branches and peered downward. Initially, all I could see were the many chub at mid-water and surface but in a slight depression between two beds of streamer weed, I spotted the tell-tale deep 'V' of a barbel's tail. My heart raced. The rest of the fish materialised, sliding into open water then ghosting back into the sanctuary of the waving streamer weed. They were still there. It looked to be around seven pounds and a beautiful fish.

I stayed watching for quite some time, mesmerised it seemed, and during that period counted five different fish moving in and out of the swim, occasionally pausing to feed on the gravelly sections, sending up small puffs of sand and disturbing a few small pebbles as they sifted for minute food particles. Totally engrossed in the antics of two smallish barbel, I gradually became aware of a large dark shape moving up alongside them. My heart beat faster and faster. This was a really big fish - the largest I had seen so far. I threw two small pieces of bait upstream of the three fish and waited. Luckily the large fish was by now ahead of the two smaller and tilted its upper lip to suck in one of the pieces as it drifted by, flaring its gills as it did so.

A large alder overhung the crystal clear water, that flowed over sand and gravel bars alternating with thick beds of streamer weed.

Stealthily, I returned to the bank, placing my large carp net in the same gap as yesterday and returned to the branches with rod in hand. I had mashed some brown bread and tossed it well upstream and beyond the barbel. The chub didn't take much tempting and were soon almost fighting over the bread as they followed it downstream, leaving the swim to the barbel, and me.

I swung the three swan shot link ledger out and very gently and slowly began to edge it along the bottom toward the fish. The first trundle through the swim resulted in me actually pulling the bait almost from the mouth of one of the smaller barbel. It took great will-power on my part, having never caught a barbel, but while there was a chance of the big fellow, that was how it would have to be. The second cast was way off mark. My shaking hands were beginning to tell and the bait passed harmlessly by, feet from the fish. I knew I had to be quick as it was only a matter of minutes perhaps before she moved through the swim to pause somewhere else, possibly out of range.

Third cast and I was spot on and edged the bait down in line with the fish's nose very slowly and as naturally as possible until it came to rest only inches away. She did not move for minutes that seemed like hours. I wondered if the vibrations of my pounding heart could be transmitted down through the branches to the roots of the tree. Any second, I expected her to drift slowly backwards, sideways, finally heading off downstream, but she just lay motionless, only the tips of those massive fins waving gently.

My arms ached, my feet ached, my whole body seemed to ache, but I dare not move, frightened the ledger would dislodge, taking with it my chance of a lifetime. Finally, with the merest movement of that gigantic tail, she slid foward, her upper lip tilting and my bait disappearing from view as she sucked it in. I honestly can't remember striking, it all happened as a blur. I just remember all hell letting loose beneath me as the fish powered off upstream and across, trying for the sanctuary of the streamer weed. The rod took on a truely alarming curve as I pointed it towards the water to side-strain the fish back towards me. It made several incredible, breathtaking runs in this manner testing the tackle to its utter limit as it dived beneath the very branches that supported me. Any second I was expecting that slackening of line, that empty, gut feeling that only anglers know, but today lady luck was smiling and I won the tug of war.

I realised it was a double and how incredibly lucky I had been.

The fish seemed played out and now came the hardest part; to descend the tree and reach the carp net. I cautiously passed the rod around the larger branches and pushed the smaller ones aside with the rod, using the weight of the fish but always maintaining pressure. It was at this point that the fish made its last bid for freedom, taking the reel handle backwards in a mad spin but it was almost spent now and I was soon in the water with the net at the ready. I waded out thigh deep once again, this time in wellingtons, receiving my second soaking in two days, but who cared with that great bronze beauty sliding towards the net?

I had to wade out even further as the branches behind me obstructed the rod as I leaned it back to net the fish, but she went in first time and I struggled back to the bank with squelching feet and laid the net gently down on the wet grass. It was only then that I saw the incredible depth of the barbel. I realised it was a double and how incredibly lucky I had been.

Weighed in the landing net at 14lbs 1oz, the net weighed 2lbs 3ozs and Norfolk's first double figure barbel was recorded at 11lbs 14ozs. I staked out the fish and after ensuring that it could remain in an upright position, rushed to the nearest phone to contact Mike at work.

"I've got one Mike!"

"You haven't!", came the reply."How big?"

"Eleven pounds fourteen ounces!"

"What do you really want?"

He just could not believe it but I finally managed to convince him and he left work immediately.

The barbel measured 27½ inches in length with a girth of 18¼ inches. Mike took several shots in black and white and colour and after a last long look, I returned her to the river. She had to be held upright for a while before finally gliding away into the depths and I watched until, blending into the shadows, she disappeared from view.

Chapter Fourteen

THERE AND BACK AGAIN

For the two seasons that followed the capture of that first barbel, I fished the Wensum but never really intensely. It seemed to me almost a crime to fish it heavily; to take advantage of the river and its barbel after they had been so obliging to me.

And so, during both the seasons that followed, I stayed in close contact with the river, doing more fish watching than fish catching but I did manage two more barbel into double figures. By now, attention was beginning to be focused upon them and inevitably the pressure increased. Local anglers were soon directing their efforts towards the barbel, closely followed by some of the country's leading specialist anglers who travelled from far and wide.

My love affair with the river and its barbel waned and rekindled with varying degrees of intensity but with the increased angling pressure, it was inevitable that my interests would, for a while, be channelled away from the river and into other directions although the barbel were now being caught on a more regular basis.

Due to their closer contact with anglers, the barbel became progressively harder to catch over the years, becoming educated to the usual baits and methods employed by most anglers and earned a reputation as being a hard fish to tempt. Several anglers fished persistently for them but few were consistently successful, many catching only one or two barbel and then calling it a day, preferring to pursue easier angling pastimes.

Consequently, angling pressure subsided somewhat and the river bank became a quieter place. In the first months of each new season it becomes increasingly difficult to get a swim on the stillwaters in the area. More and more, anglers seem to turn their backs on the rivers to pursue carp and tench. On the river, swims are always free. It seems almost as if river angling is becoming a somewhat forgotten art with today's modern anglers.

So, in the mid 1980s, I returned to the Wensum to pursue the barbel once again. My first full season back on the river, fishing purely for barbel and I learnt and re-learnt the

The two seasons that followed, I managed barbel into double figures.

Barbel country.

basics. One problem I encountered once more was that I found searching for, and observing barbel, almost as enjoyable as actually fishing for them. It is a problem I will never solve. Many's the time I have dragged myself from a vantage point inside a bush or nestled within the branches of a tree to start fishing before the evening turned to night. But location is all important as with all forms of angling and I would rather spend three hours searching and one hour fishing, in the knowledge that I had fish in the swim.

I caught eight fish during that summer of long, unhurried evenings. The largest at 10lbs 9ozs, notable for its blind eye. Another larger barbel was lost at the net but that as they say, is all in the game and all in all, I was very pleased with my season. Conventional baits such as corn and meat had proven effective but in slightly different variants due to the wariness of the barbel.

The following season initially proved not so easy. I carried on from where I had left off the previous year trying hard with the same methods and baits but the barbel were having none of it! It is typical of fish whatever the species. Just when you think you are getting somewhere, they change their habits and you are left to scratch your head and wonder where to start once again. There's nowt so queer as fish.

By July, I had caught only two barbel and one had been an encounter full of doubts and perhaps the tale deserves telling in more detail.

Chapter Fifteen

A DOUBTFUL ENCOUNTER

Thursday evening, another hectic day over and I looked forward to the peace of the evening session by the river. I headed the car homeward and after a quick meal and a change of clothing, was soon on my way toward the Wensum. Swinging the car off the road into the makeshift car park, I recognised the estate car of my old friend Dave Humphries. He was down for a quiet evening on the river with Charles Beane, away from the hustle and bustle of the local stillwaters.

After a brief chat about what had been caught and what hadn't, I left them to their fishing and began the usual nightly ritual of 'find the barbel', hoping that they would be in one or more of my prepared swims. Starting from the high vantage point within the branches of the tree in 'the Copse', I could view a wide area that had recently become popular with a group of medium sized barbel; but not tonight. Only a few chub worrying some crusts that had drifted down from the mill along with their wrapper. The swirls disturbed the still air as they knocked into the bread, taking small pieces as it slowly sank and not directly from the surface. They know all about floating crust, these wily old Wensum chub.

I perched there uncomfortably for about half an hour in the vain hope that the group of barbel would move in but finally, with stiff limbs, I descended and moved upstream to the next swims. The lack of bankside trees and shrubbery here made spotting difficult and I made a promise to try this area from the other, higher bank. I peered into 'the Telegraph swim', I scanned 'the Shallows', but the barbel were playing hard to get and even harder to see. I was sure I had passed some fish over but in the overcast conditions, the light was fading early and I hurried on to the very topmost swims.

The 'Top swim' was almost totally obscured by a gigantic weed raft from the recent cutting operation of the River Authority upstream. I hoped they would miss this section as they sometimes had in the past and leave the barbel and chub to spawn in peace.

Thankfully, the most difficult swim to fish from this bank, 'the Aquarium', inside the alder bushes, was barren of fish as was the swim I call 'Snag 1', apart from the inevitable and voracious chub. That left only one final swim that could be viewed effectively from my bank - 'Snag 2'. But this was no easy swim to look into.

By now the light had almost gone into the twilight of the evening and the bats were flittering overhead. If I did not find them here, it would mean taking pot luck and fishing a swim blind; something I did not particularly want to do. As I squelched through the thick mud that lay under several inches of moving water, pushing my way deeper into the dense thicket, I wondered if a number of the barbel had moved off downstream as they usually did at this time of the season. But I was sure not all of them had deserted this, their most favoured area.

As the branches thinned near the water's edge, I crept as stealthily as possible, the mud still tugging at my waders, until I reached a point where I could push aside the few remaining leafy twigs and observe the swim in detail. The fast current pushed almost noiselessly by the trailing branches to my right where another debris raft had accumulated. Between this and the slack to my left lay the long gravel run and it was here, towards the tail end, that the shadows moved. It was still very difficult to see clearly but I was sure they were there. Chub were very active all about the swim, coming up so close that had I leaned down, I could easily have touched their backs. The dark shadows, almost beyond viewing range due to the surface glare, moved only slowly and purposefully. I knew they were barbel; they just had to be.

I stayed, trying not to sink any deeper into the mud, hoping for a definite confirmation with the mosquitoes buzzing and the swallows still skimming. I glanced away from the river, fascinated by the antics of an acrobatic water rat as it scurried along a branch close overhead and as my eyes returned to the river, the confirmation lay at my feet. A barbel of perhaps 6lbs feeding leisurely in the sandy mud, sending out wispy clouds that were soon pushed away with the current. Almost out of sight, I could make out another large shape, either two small barbel or one very large fish. I hoped it was the latter but either way, the quest was over for tonight and I waited for the barbel close in to move on before putting in a few handfulls of hemp that soon were spreading and sinking along the length of the gravel run.

A thin, ghostly mist hung in the air just above the fields on the far bank, the railway bridge now a black silhouette against the sky. Peacocks called their wailing lament from Blake's aviary beyond the fields to my left and I made my first cast over the swim, drawing back the baited hook until I felt the lead scrape on gravel. I doubted if the lobworm would have much peace as the dusk turned to blackness and the rod was soon knocking with the attentions of the eels. Two eels later and I began to worry that this activity would scare off my hard found fish. Another approach was called for. The barbel were often spooked by corn but I wondered if only a hookbait over the hemp bed might be taken. At least I could have another cup of coffee in peace.

Dave and Charles had had enough and paused for another chat on their way back to the car. Crouching close behind me, we talked of tench and carp, the absence of barbel and how their seasons had progressed. I kept an eye on the rod tip as I finished the coffee and began to think of a recast further down the gravel run.

9.45pm and the rod tip, curving slightly towards the upstream ledger, quivered, relaxed momentarily and then wrenched over violently. A fish was on and I waded out holding hard to prevent it travelling further upstream, into the trailing branches of the thicket from where I had probably observed it earlier. The pressure held it then relaxed as the

fish came downstream and I regained line only to lose it once more as it retraced its path into the centre of the river where I knew it to be clear of weed and snags. I allowed it to go, back-winding under pressure and followed the curve of the rod against the sky as it moved again downstream well within the clear area. But it continued to go and I really had to pile on the pressure, side-straining the fish into the slacker water at my bank where it ploughed about doggedly for several minutes.

Dave shone a torch on the surface as it neared the net. A huge tail broke surface as Charles sunk the net and I walked slowly back. Whether it was the torch or the net, or both, the barbel panicked and tore off again downstream, embedding itself in the thick weed below the gravel. I slackened off and

changed the angle of pressure and after a brief pause, the fight was resumed and I regained line, finally drawing her into the shallows and the torchbeam again as Charles netted it successfully at the second attempt.

I followed the line down to the hook and in the torchlight, elation turned to dismay. The hook was almost two inches outside the mouth, held only by a tiny sliver of skin. We made a close inspection of the mouth which revealed a long red scrape inside that could have been made by an insecure, slipping hook hold. I doubted that such a tiny sliver of skin could have held for the duration of the battle, considering all the heavy pressure that I had exerted on the fish. The hook may have moved during the fight, as the fish snagged, even in the net, or not at all. I would never know for certain but after a few photographs by flashlight and recording a weight of 11lbs 6ozs, we left her to recuperate for almost half an hour in the folds of the large landing net.

She swam away slowly and strongly but did not go far, laying close into the bank in the clear, shallow water. I packed away my gear, reflecting on the recent events and just before leaving, I shone my torch once again into the margins. The barbel had not moved and I reached down to gently touch its tail. With an annoyed shake, she slowly moved off across the shallows, into the deeper water and I held her in the torchbeam until, reaching the first barrier of streamer weed, she gave an extra thrust of the tail and was gone.

I switched off the torch and the silent darkness of the riverbank again enveloped me as I made my way through the dense undergrowth, back to the car and home.

Chapter Sixteen

NEW IDEAS

During the sessions that followed, I began to experience bites that either did not develop or were unhitable. It was probably all in my mind; one of those desparate periods that all big-fish anglers endure, when fish are few and far between. The abortive bites could have been chub or eels but I was convinced that the swims I had baited were frequented by barbel at sometime during the evening. I had even seen them feeding on occasion so I must have been doing something wrong. The time was ripe for some experimentation with baits and methods. I had nothing to lose.

Hemp, as always, provided an excellent attractor and I had limited success fishing the single grain of corn over a bed of hemp but, as with hemp as a hookbait, it still seemed rather a 'needle in a haystack' situation. Corn and meat were soon disregarded as baits. I had seen the barbel bolt at the sight of them on several occasions. There was always the odd fish that would pick up these baits but I was not prepared to wait that long for just one or two fluke fish. Natural baits such as worms and maggots were a much better proposition apart from their eel and chub catching abilities; but once this was endured, the barbel came increasingly to net. I also experimented with pastes with varying degrees of success but other species still remained a problem. The eels and chub, I found, acted as an excellent pointer to barbel activity. If they fed well, the barbel would not be far behind. Eel and chub activity would often lull as the barbel moved in, probably attracted from downstream by the disturbed sediment and food particles. But there was sometimes a fish that would defy all the rules and take a bait viciously when you were least expecting it and least prepared.

As for bite detection, Barbel anglers have probably used the rod tip as indicator for centuries and I was not about to question this infinite wisdom until, after suffering many unproductive bites on the rod tip and quivertip, I became increasingly disallusioned. Firstly, I was sure that not all barbel gave the unmistakable, thumping great wrench that almost tears arm from socket. Secondly, without a truely confident bite it was extremely difficult to know when to strike effectively. Usually too early, (I should have left it!) or too late, (I should have hit it!) Finally, I became sure that some fish could feel the rod or quivertip and were leaving the bait if they had not removed it from the hook, as was often the case with soft baits such as worm or paste.

I needed a new method of bite detection. Something akin to touch ledgering but without all the effort during the long hours of inactivity. A method that would give the fish a little slack line before it felt any resistance at all.

I began to experiment with several ideas and finally settled for an almost stillwater approach. With this method, a single rod is positioned as parallel as possible to the riverbank, undergrowth permitting, pointing downstream in two rod rests directly at the bait. With the tip close to the surface, the rod is always held, or rather rested upon, as some barbel bites can be incredibly vicious affairs. During one session, I turned to reach for a flask and found my rod straining and pivoting on the front rest, the rod butt high in the air, reel handle spinning wildly as a barbel charged off downstream finally ejecting bait and hook. (Awarded 'The Barbel Bite of the Season'!)

A betalight is attached to the rod tip and another in a 'monkey climber' situated beneath the butt ring and second ring. A bobbin can be used instead of the 'monkey' but I prefer the latter as the tension of the 'monkey' on its needle is just sufficient to counter the pull of a summer current.

It is facinating to watch a barbel bite develop on this set-up and proves that barbel do not always just grab the bait and run. Firstly the line where it enters the water will begin to tremble. Seconds pass, the tip begins to rock gently. (Hence the betalight on the tip.) These vibrations can all be felt whilst holding the rod and are followed either by the 'monkey' moving up the needle so fast it is not visible or, and this is not uncommon, a slow confident bite, the 'monkey' finally flying off as the strike is made, sometimes never reaching the top.

With the new approach to baits and bite indication, my catch rate began to improve dramatically. On the first evening in mid August, using a combination of different baits and the new method I caught three barbel in a session. Something I had not done before. I continued to fish for them until the end of September as the summer drew to a close. By then I had taken fish of 9lbs 10ozs, two at 9lbs 3ozs, 8lbs 6ozs, 8lbs 3ozs, 7lbs 10ozs and several others at five and six pounds; the smallest, a completely perfect example of its species, 5lbs 6ozs.

A new approach

But the truely huge fish for which the Wensum is so justly famous eluded my endeavours that summer and into autumn. Catching barbel of any size during those tranquil evenings on the river was reward enough and these results were very encouraging. There was always next season for the big fish and as I developed my method and expanded my knowledge of swims, baits and barbel behaviour, little did I expect it all to culminate in the dramatic turn of events that following summer.

Chapter Seventeen

SEASON OF SUCCESS

As the close season draws to an end, the garden is finally in good order. The house has been cared for, maintained and redecorated, the brushes cleaned and put away for another nine months. The children have been spoilt on so many outings, but in between, some time has been stolen for repairs to rods and reels. Line has been renewed, hooks sharpened, tackle boxes replenished and generally tidied.

Close season weather is often kind; sunny and dry. Ideal for occasionally putting the river into a low and clear condition that makes fish spotting so easy and enjoyable. Old and favourite areas have been visited and probably some new ones found. The reactions of barbel and chub to baits have been tested at close quarters and theories formed. But this information can sometimes be dangerously unreliable. Fish will feed on anything with gay abandon during the close season. After June 16th, they become very much more selective.

The weather always seems to change as May moves into June and as the new season approached, it was going to be no exception. The skies had been heavy and a dark, battleship grey for days, the rain and wind painting a dull, moisture laden landscape. I expected the main sluice to be pushing hard into the weirpool, the river up and coloured, and so it was on the evening of June 14th, but only by inches and still easily fishable. This visit to the river did nothing to prepare me for the shock as I reached it once again on the following day.

Late afternoon, John Bailey and I had battled our way through the towering forest of nettles, across the flood plain and gaped in astonishment as the river came into view. Now a raging torrent of thick, milk chocolate brown, speckled with the bright greens of weed torn away by the power of the flood. Just breaking its banks, we watched as the river rose about our feet and we quickly changed our plans for the first night of the new season.

As fast as the river had risen, it began to fall and within twenty four hours was once again fishable, if with some difficulty. The river, for now, retained its hue and spotting barbel in the coloured water was out of the question, so as evening approached, I settled for my favourite and most productive swim of last year. I felt confident here and eager to cast. After baiting the swim carefully, I walked upstream, letting things settle down and finding out what changes the sudden flood-water had made to the other swims along my bank.

I returned at around 5.30pm, the weather now clear but cool for mid June with a summer breeze rattling the leaves above me and rustling through the reeds along the far bank. The swallows skimmed, the insects buzzed and the sweet, earthy smell of the summer river was all about. The first cast, I gently lobbed out under-arm and held back as the link ledger and lobtail entered the water almost silently, the gentle ripples flowing downstream on the current. Activity was almost immediate as several positive pulls plucked nervously at the indicator. Fish were obviously responsible and feeding over

John Bailey visited the swim and offered to take a photograph.

my carefully laid carpet of bait. It remained to be seen if any of them had whiskers!

At 6.05pm, a bite very gradually developed into a slow, confident lift that I contacted just before the indicator reached the top of the needle and the first barbel of the new season, always a very special fish, was reminding me just how hard its species could fight. At 7lbs 7ozs, a welcome start and as the fish recovered in the landing net, John Bailey visited the swim to see how I was faring and offered to take a photograph.

The barbel was returned further upstream and as we talked, I topped up the swim with more bait. John had fished the top of the stretch but had to leave early due to work commitments and as he wished me luck and disappeared into the undergrowth, I recast and settled back once again. Almost and hour had passed since the first barbel and as John's car started up in the car park, the rod tip once again knocked, the indicator twitched nervously then moved straight up the needle quite fast. The session was definitely beginning to warm up as I found myself connected to the second barbel of the evening. This latest fish came in like a lamb after its first mad rush, the line tangling around one of the pelvic fins, the hook embedding itself almost to the eye in one side of the lower lip.

The Avon scales settled at 8lbs 14ozs, an immaculate bronze beauty, almost scale perfect and much deserving of a photograph. I quickly rigged up my camera on the tripod and took one picture of each side for the angling diary.

Around 7.40pm, a small chub of maybe two pounds put in an appearance and it seemed the swim had not only barbel but several chub competing for my free feed. Between them they must certainly have been mopping up, feeding ravenously in the river conditions they loved; a river fining down with plenty of colour and even more food.

After the small chub, I returned home quickly, leaving my tackle, to collect more bait and by the time I restarted, a little after 9.15pm, the dusk was slowly creeping in. Across the river, the treeline beyond the field gradually turned from green to a stark black silhouette lightened only by the mist from the valley. The bats replaced the swallows, the insects gaining little respite from the darkness. I watched spellbound as one bat, probably a Pipesstrelle, skimmed the river twice taking tiny sips of water, its wings translucent in the last glow before the sun finally faded completely from the sky.

I had just settled back and another suicide chub of two pounds disturbed my swim. I wondered if it was the same fish I had taken earlier as I carefully returned him, hoping he would tell his friends to keep away for tonight. 10.35pm and it was now totally dark, the breeze had died and it seemed warmer. The green glow of the indicator moved slowly to the top of the needle and the tremors of erratic vibrations passed along the rod to my hand as I struck instinctively. But I connected only with the branches behind me as the link ledger whistled dangerously past my ear.

After fifteen minutes, another bite began to develop almost imperceptibley. It seemed as if I could almost feel the fish moving towards the baited hook and my grip tightened on the rod as I imagined the loose feed gradually disappearing, the fish coming closer and closer, its fins and body moving slowly, brushing the line slightly until finally, the hookbait a blur, it moved fast between the fishes lips as it was sucked powerfully backwards.

It is not often easy playing a large river fish in the unreal surroundings of darkness with snags and weedbeds that seem so much larger than during daylight, only feet away. This particular adversary was no exception. Whether from my heavy persuasion or of its own accord, the fish fortunately moved upstream and I breathed a silent sigh of relief, playing it out in the relatively clear area immediately in front of me, beyond my screen of reeds. In the blackness I netted the commotion rather than the fish and as I admired and inspected it in the dim torchlight I realised it was of a very similar size to the previous barbel. One ounce less in fact and it was possible I had captured the same unfortunate individual again but studying the photographs later, it was obvious that they were different fish, if perhaps from the same year class.

Three barbel in one session and the gods were smiling. Everything seemed just right and I was determined to take advantage of this ideal situation, intending to fish throughout the night, but by 12.15am the swim had died completely. I decided to call it a day and return in the morning, putting in my remaining bait, preparing the swim for the dawn session only a short summer's night away.

It was raining quite heavily as I returned, making my way through the dripping undergrowth in the twilight but my enthusiasm was not dampened, the memory of the previous evening still fresh in my mind. Only four hours had passed and I was soon settled beneath the umbrella with the drumming of the rain to keep me company. Unexpectedly, the skies cleared and I enjoyed a beautiful sunrise, bright, calm and misty, although the air was still quite chilling. The trees and bushes all around continued to shed their water in drips and rivulets, aided by the faintest of breezes. The morning session followed roughly the same pattern as the previous evening and, as usual, I jotted down the times and events in my diary as they occured.

4.15am - Start.

4.25am - Small chub. Very slow, twitchy bite.

5.50am - A very fast bite. Terrific battle. Snagged me once to the right under the tree branches but I banged the rod butt several times and the fish moved out but continued to fight extremely hard. I thought it was enormous. *The* one, but it was not to be. Only 5lbs 6ozs but welcome nevertheless. (Half of right hand gill cover missing.) It just goes to prove that when you lose that unseen monster, you very rarely have. It's just a small one playing tricks and having some fun.

6.25am - Rod knocked for a long while before the indicator shot up fast. Again fought very well, especially under the rod tip and just would not come to net. 8lbs exactly. (Tip of dorsal fin curved over towards the tail.)

9.00am I packed up as all now very quiet for some time. The brief, bright dawn now deteriorated back to an even cooler and overcast day with a chill breeze bringing a promise of more summer rain to top up the river.

At 8lbs 14ozs, an immaculate bronze beauty, almost scale perfect.

The capture of one further barbel from the swim of 7lbs 10ozs, signified an end to activity there and in all probability meant that I had caught or disturbed the majority of the small shoal of barbel that had made this their temporary home. I began to search new areas as the river continued to clear, where I had not previously seen or caught barbel; but it proved to be not the easiest of tasks.

Only three short weeks had passed by and the river was now much lower than on opening night. It still carried some colour but the chocolate brown had faded to a weak, milkless tea. In the shallower areas, with the help of an hour or two of sunlight, fish could be seen and I searched along several stretches, looking in the most unlikely of places as well as the most obvious, determined to carry on until I was successful.

In the hundred yards or so of river bank broken by alders, hawthorn, reeds and the occasional small oak on my bank, I was sure that some barbel, large or small, must be present. But as I moved upstream, gradually eliminating the

All that Summer, flood seemed to follow flood.

126

areas that could be viewed from the trees, bushes and slightly higher banks, I had seen only streamer weed, chub and one solitary and lonely tench, heading purposefully downstream, perhaps in a vain search for others of its kind. It could even have been a refugee from 'the pond by the mill'.

Into the last section and I became increasingly resigned to failure as I gently eased myself once again into the branches of another tree that hung perilously close over the water. I pulled my old, battered hat down, shading the polariods and strained my eyes to see through the tinged water to the bottom. A long, shallow, sandy glide gradually deepened beneath the branches and the water darkened, broken by outcrops of weed that waved enticingly in the current. Between them, other long, dark, stationary patches occurred over the sandy river bed and I began to get interested, my suspicions immediately aroused.

Several snub-nosed chub passed through the swim at mid-water with their characteristic body movement, not

pausing, heading upstream for some unknown destination. But my stare remained fixed, waiting for a tell-tale, give-away sign from the dark, shadowy shapes. A movement or a flash of bronze from the depths. It is uncanny how weed will sway in the current, the perfect imitation of stationary fish holding their own against the flow.

Minutes passed. Maybe they were not barbel after all. Just clever weed patches. I was not totally convinced either way and began to get uncomfortable in the branches. Then - Bingo! A flash of gold as one of the 'weed patches' twisted its side to the sunlight, returning to the river bed to become just another long, dark shadow. Had I blinked, I probably would have missed it and shortly moved on. As it was, I counted them. Five in all. Still vague shapes but other movements became more obvious the longer I watched and one in particular seemed quite large.

I knew I should have baited the swim for several nights, leaving the barbel to build up their confidence on my free offerings but I was just too impatient, always in a hurry to get nowhere. I didn't know if the swim was a long term holding area or whether they were just passing through. Here today, gone tomorrow. So, that evening from 8pm until midnight, I fished and caught only one chub and that on the first cast. It didn't even give me a chance to put the indicator on the line and had probably disturbed the swim from that point on.

The next two evenings followed in much the same fashion. The barbel were still there on occasion. The third evening I watched one very large fish from the tree, moving over the shallows, feeding occasionally and actively searching for food. I persevered but doubts crowded in. Still no barbel had come to net from a swim obviously very popular with them. I must have been missing something.

Then on the forth evening, events took on a dramatic turn. The constant baiting while I fished over the three evenings finally took effect as the shoal lost its caution and accepted my presence and the unnatural carpet of free food. It would mean their downfall.

By the end of the fourth evening session I was glad that I had persevered. The barbel had finally fed and fed hard during an evening of bright sunshine cooled by a strong westerly wind.

The continuous twitching of the indicator betrayed their presence (or that of the chub), from the very outset and it was not long before I struck into something of considerable power that ran upstream into heavy weed, depositing hook and tackle there before I had a chance to do anything about it. First round to 'them!'

Only minutes later I was playing another unseen force that once again ran upstream as I contacted it but this time I was more successful. There must have been over twelve pounds in the landing net as I dragged it onto the bank, but unfortunately only six pounds one ounce of the total weight was barbel, the rest being a substantial part of the nearby weedbed.

Just over a hour passed so quickly. 9.30pm, the brightness had gone from the evening and another barbel headed off very fast upstream as I answered an incredibly fast bite that had cracked the monkey climber into the rod. I cursed hard that I had not set the needle low enough.

Obviously, a better fish this time, I could tell from its power and the thrashing of water. It wallowed heavily, like a bathing pig, as it neared the bank, a white belly silhouetted against the black surface. But swimming upstream had been an unwise manoeuvre and I soon had it secure in the net. 9lbs 3ozs of perfect barbel beauty and symmetry sometimes not seen in the larger fish, every fin and scale perfect.

Two hours passed and no other barbel or signs of their presence, only a smallish chub, so at 11.30pm I reeled in, baited the swim for the morning and left.

Morning sessions are only rarely as productive as those in the evening and so it proved but even the following three evening sessions were disappointing. Chub and eels fed well on my offerings but for all that time I had caught only one further barbel of 6lbs and lost another. The line had either been cut near the hook on some sharp underwater obstacle or I had been bitten off.

It once again became increasingly difficult to see into the Wensum. Intermittent rain showers, some heavy, had coloured the water. Shadows were present but even more indisernable and nothing was certain. Perhaps the main shoal had moved on, leaving one or two stragglers. Perhaps I should move on.

Another puzzle that began to intrigue me was why many of the fish I had caught ran upstream when first hooked. Had they all come to some strange underwater agreement to make my life easier? Did they intend that I should hit more bites and land more fish? Something finally clicked in my mind. I had an uncomfortable feeling that realisation should have dawned much earlier, but when it came it was like a penny dropping into a tin mug. They were running upstream because I made them!

It became clearer the more I thought about it and I knew I could take advantage of this newly found bonus of knowledge. I was fishing from the left hand bank looking downstream, the rod placed almost parallel to the bank pointing downstream. When I struck it was to the left away from the river and as I did so the hook was pulled into the near side of the barbel's mouth as the fish pointed upstream.

Striking to the left in this way also meant hitting more bites. It was logical, an upstream strike to the right would often wrench bait and hook directly from the front of a fishes' mouth before it had gained a hold.

Feeling pressure from the side and not directly from the front, the fish did the obvious thing. It bolted forward in the direction it was pointing, away from other fish in the swim, away from downstream snags and the help of the current and weed flow, past me to where I could handle all eventualities with far greater ease.

Once I had realised what was happening, the baiting pattern was also modified to extract as much as possible from the situation. Instead of just 'an area' of bait concentrating the shoal with my hookbait in the centre, I placed it into a long thin strip that the barbel, now spread out, would move along. By placing my baited hook at the very top of this strip, I could pick off the furthest upstream fish and get it out of the feeding area, away from the rest of the shoal before they too were spooked.

The next evening I decided to start in a different swim perhaps thirty yards downstream. It was very windy and I was glad I no longer had to rely on a quiver tip for bite indication. A continuous grey bank of cloud blotted out the sun and trying to spot even shadows in the murky water was impossible. At least it was a warm wind but the constant fine drizzle, that soaked everything without really trying, did nothing to raise the spirits.

This new swim held great promise. Deep and gravel bottomed, it was overhung by a profusion of alder bushes, the current pushing through fast near the surface. Deep below it was much slower and to my mind an ideal place where barbel might linger and perhaps feed.

I stayed there for an hour and a half and it was not disallusionment with the swim that made me move. It was a nagging voice from inside my head saying,

"You shouldn't be here!"

And so, always one to follow instinct, I had to move. But to where? The answer was obvious and by 9pm I was back in the usual swim and for some reason, brimming with confidence. This new feeling was well founded as the indicator was active from the beginning, keeping me on edge and alert with constant jerks and plucks.

Five minutes past ten and the illuminous green glow was there one minute and gone the next. It had been a very poor cast, to far to the left and not far enough downstream but no-one had informed the barbel. I had no recollection of seeing the indicator move but can remember trying to struggle to my feet with a pulsating rod straining first upstream and then abruptly downstream as the fish made a sudden about turn.

With incredible strength it powered further down using the current and I followed it as far as possible until confronted by a wall of bushes. Leaning perilously over the river I could only stand my ground and feel the curve of the rod increasing dangerously as the fish exerted ever more pressure. Something had to give and I prayed it would be the fish and fortunately they were answered.

Pressure eased off as the power of the rod took effect, turning the fish over, and I tried to regain line as quickly as possible while I had the upper hand and before the barbel had time to regain its composure.

But regain it, it did, rocketing off downstream again, the procedure having to be repeated once more. It was as the line was being regained for the second time that all went solid. The fish had found sanctuary in the weed, probably pulled there by the strange but irresistible force from upstream.

I could still feel the tugging vibrations as I slackened off, but the harder I pulled back, the more solid it all became. I had walked as far downstream as possible, so turning the rod over, I changed the direction of pull. Very gradually there was some give at the tip, then slowly all came free. The fish felt slower and heavier now, due to a blanket of weed pulling down heavily on the line and I was glad of the help to counter the final surges as the fish slowly tired.

Eventually, it was almost in the net but fish and weed were too much for the frame and it spun on the handle, the fish thrashing the surface into spray as it made off once again. I made no such mistake at the second attempt and as I parted fish from weed and net I knew it was over ten pounds. 29¼ inches long and 17 inches in girth, it weighed 10lbs 8 ozs and I felt like kissing it but instead, contented myself with a quiet shout across the river.

I shall recognise her again if we should meet. One gill cover was deformed, an area missing but apart from that and a split pelvic fin there were no other abnormalities, her appetite certainly not adversely affected.

Needless to say, I was back again the next evening and settled in the swim by 8pm. The weather was a repeat performance of the previous night even down to the fine drizzle. The level of the river remained high but it seemed to be clearing once again.

By 10pm I had caught two chub, missed a slow bite and one real humdinger while reaching for the flask. Ten minutes passed so slowly as I held the rod tight, now keyed up, knowing that something was about to happen. I was not to be disappointed as a few sharp pulls plucked at the monkey on its needle. There was a pause as all remained motionless. It seemed an age but was probably only minutes until finally another humdinger of a bite that I just knew I was not going to miss.

The battle raged with neither opponent gaining the upper hand and keeping it. Line see-sawed through the rings as I retrieved it only to lose it once again but inevitably the fish began to tire, staying deep and slow, without the wild rushes that had characterised the beginning of the fight. I pumped the fish upward and a silhouetted link ledger broke the surface followed by vortices that were carried away on the current.

Again I almost had the fish netted, but it found new strength and dived to the left, deep and fast, keeping very close in. She was tired now and the heavy pressure from almost directly above returned her abruptly to the surface and back into the waiting net. It was a strain lifting such weight over the reeds and obvious that this was another good fish.

Almost the first feature I noticed reflecting back in the dim torchlight was a very distinctive tail fin. It was the same fish as my 'Doubtful Encounter' of the previous summer, this time without any doubts. Well and truely hooked just inside the left hand corner of the mouth and weighing exactly the same as a year ago.

I fished on until almost 1am without further event and walked back across the field, the stars now breaking through the cloud cover, smiling down on a happy man.

In the morning over breakfast, I informed the family of how my evening session had developed. They were very

The same fish as my 'Doubtful Encounter' of the previous summer.

pleased but perhaps I would stay at home tonight. Sim knew better. A ten pounder on the first night, an eleven pounder on the second night, I must go back and capture a twelve pounder on the third night she insisted! I was already convinced. I didn't for one minute think that I would come anywhere near to realising the dream, this run of luck must end soon.

But at 8.30pm that next evening, after only an hour in the swim, I found myself vainly trying to subdue the irresistible power of an express train that had attached itself to my line. Taking the now familiar path, it headed upstream and just went and went and went. There was no choice in the matter, I just had to let it go, the eight pound Maxima line suddenly seemed totally inadequate. The line was given grudgingly, every inch payed for in expended energy and effort, the reel handle back-winding furiously.

At the end of this first run, I finally stopped the fish, turning it on the surface. The crash of water sounded like thunder in the still of the evening. (I paced out the distance of this first run later at almost forty yards.) She came downstream protestingly and neared the net three times before eventually sulking just beyond the rod tip, thumping and pulling it down towards the surface. This time, there was no fiasco with the net. I had changed over to using a large carp net and the barbel was soon safely engulfed.

Hooked once again in the left hand side of the mouth (viewed head-on) it reinforced my theories, missing the dream by merely an ounce but I was fully satisfied and found it hard to continue fishing, packing up at the early hour of 10pm.

It had taken ten years to better my best barbel and then only by an ounce, but it seemed unimportant. I couldn't remember when I had enjoyed my fishing so much. But it was not all good news. I was impatient to see the photographs and as I tried to wind back the film, I knew that disaster had struck. The film with my largest ever barbel on it had not wound on! I was devastated but its no good crying over unexposed film. I would just have to catch the fish again!

It had rained heavily during the following day and the river was higher with a good tinge of colour, a warm breeze replacing the strong wind. The barbel loved these conditions and I landed two of them; 9lbs 1oz and 6lbs ½oz and missed another cracker of a bite.

An early start the next evening did me little good. I had to wait until 11.10pm, after missing two good bites, before I contacted another fish. 10lbs 1oz; a beautiful barbel with a distinctive tailfin that fought so incredibly hard.

Then, at 12.20am, the impossible happened. A fish headed upstream so fast and for so long, I didn't think it would ever stop. It was déjà vu - a repeat performance of the camera-shy 11lbs 15oz fish and it was not really surprising.

Once in the net, I noticed the big tail, the hefty girth and recognised the split dorsal. It *was* the 11.15, this time weighing three ounces less. Two doubles in one session and I made sure the film wound on this time!

I fished the swim three more evenings but it became evident that the main shoal had either moved on or wised up, only one other barbel of 5lbs 4ozs resulting. I certainly couldn't complain. The river had once again been very kind to me with five double figure barbel over five evenings.

It was time for a move. I baited another swim for four nights and on the fifth evening, extracted three barbel from it to 9lbs 7ozs before having to leave at the early hour of 10.20pm due to the imminent appearance of Harper Minimus number three at any moment.

By the first of August, he still hadn't appeared and so I chanced another short session and it seemed my luck still hadn't run out - 10lbs 3ozs.

But that was that; enough was enough. So many big barbel began to seem a little like too much chocolate cake and family responsibilities were pressing. There were other species to fish for after all, before summer drifted into autumn.

It missed the dream by merely an ounce.

137

Chapter Eighteen

THE BARREL

Even from my earliest fishing days, chub had often lured me to the banks of the Wensum. After 1977 and my baptism of fire with the Wensum barbel, the chub were somewhat eclipsed in my angling interests and it was not until fairly recently that one chub rekindled the old flame.

I had spent the dawn at the carp lake but by lunchtime, had tired of waiting for indicators that always obeyed the laws of gravity. I stopped by the river on my way home, hoping to pin-point some barbel for the evening session and bait a few swims with hemp.

Many years had passed since the old willow had been felled below the point. An impressive alder had grown to take its place and overlook the river in the same area; time as always the greatest of healers.

This alder overlooks a gravel run that, in early season, is quite extensive. As the summer progresses and weed growth proliferates, the swim becomes smaller and smaller until finally, by the autumn, it is almost unfishable unless by surface or sub-surface methods. It seems the fish prefer it open as it is only favoured in early season and it was at just such a time that I first encountered 'The Barrel'.

The day remained cloudy but the river was crystal clear. Even before I settled in the alder tree, as I climbed through the branches, I could easily see the many chub that had taken up residence in this swim.

I watched them, not really taking too much notice at first as I could see no barbel, until I spotted what I thought was a carp at the tail end of the swim, stationary and dwarfing all the chub, it lay below, nestled almost on the bottom. Carp are not uncommon along some stretches of the Wensum. Indeed, several lengths are quite heavily populated with mirrors and some commons that have escaped from the fish farm at Hellesdon during extremely high water levels, so I was not surprised.

But in this instance I was wrong. It definitely was no carp! As I watched, the fish began to move about the swim and even appeared at the surface giving me a very clear view and showing itself to be an exceptional and extremely large chub. So bulky in fact that it didn't seem to be swimming on an even keel.

Although the season was still young, it seemed late for a chub to have retained spawn. Perhaps it was diseased or spawn bound or perhaps it was just a freak of nature, it certainly looked healthy enough; a giant chub just waiting to make its appearance in the angling weeklies.

There was no need for decisions. I must have a try for this beast of a fish and returned to the car for some tackle. A carp rod would have to do as would the net. Six pound breaking strain line was more in keeping but bait proved a problem. I doubted that my carp baits, whatever the flavour, would really do the trick. A rummage through the remains of my lunch box produced a drying sandwich. Perhaps that was all I needed.

I returned to the branches of the tree, rod and

sandwich in hand, having left the ridiculously large carp net at its base. Questions, as always, crowded in. Could I get the bait through the mass of smaller chub? Would I land it from high within the tree? Would it take a bait? Was it still there?

I scanned the swim intently. Yes, there she was. Still deep but having moved slightly upstream, now positioned more favourably, just down from where my rod tip would soon be.

Putting the two halves of the rod together, I baited the number eight, 'Jack Hilton' hook with a small piece of flake from the sandwich remains. It was not easy, the bread being not quite moist enough now, but I had little choice. It would have to do.

There were perhaps a dozen other chub in the swim to well over four pounds but they all paled to insignificance by comparison with the one that stole my attentions. I realised I was trembling in anticipation, the first time for a very long while that a chub had made me this excited! But I must be patient. The majority of the chub were at the surface or sub-surface and very mobile. They would swim slowly from one end of the swim upstream to reach its head then cut

140

across river and down to come back into the tail end of the gravel run and repeat the procedure once again.

If I timed it correctly, I could put a bait to the big fish with a minimum of competition. My chance came after perhaps forty-five minutes. The bulk of the chub had left the swim on their circuit patrol. 'The Barrel' still remained, accompanied by two smaller consorts; one of perhaps two and a half pounds, the other close to four pounds.

I swung the single swan shot and baited hook through the leaves, out of the branches and let it drop silently into the flow a couple of yards or so above the fish. I had anticipated a wait of some time but the fishes' reaction, all three of them, was instantaneous. They all made a beeline for my bait, a speck of white that stood out so clearly against the gravel. I can remember thinking,

"Yes, here we go. The smallest is sure to get to the bait first".

But I was wrong. It was 'The Barrel', bullying the other two out of the way and in an instant my bait was in her mouth and I leaned heavily on the rod, bracing myself for a strong vicious pull from below, whilst hanging onto the tree for dear life with the other arm. But there was nothing! I connected only with fresh air as the swan shot lost itself with a crash into the leaves just below me and in desperate disappointment, I silently cursed the fish, fishing, life itself!

My imperfect flake bait had, in an instant, been sucked clear from the hook a split second before I had struck. 'The Barrel' and her entourage were well and truly spooked. They headed downstream in no uncertain terms to be soon lost from sight in amongst the streamer weed, quickly replaced by the other chub having now completed yet another circuit.

I watched the swim for hours after, and searched others, hoping she would return but I was to be disappointed and so went home, returning in the evening armed with moist, fresh bread, lobworms, corn and a variety of other chub styled goodies.

And incredibly, as I climbed the tree once again that evening there she was, almost the first chub I saw. I couldn't believe my luck. A second attempt, a second chance to go for gold and after only a short wait for the 'circuit' chub to move out, I was soon swinging out a piece of moist flake towards the fish. And once again, the action ended in an instant. Even as the single swan shot sunk the highly visible bait, small chub seemed to come from nowhere and were upon it. This time 'The Barrel' was not the fastest and I pulled the bait from the lips of a small chub of around two pounds but the damage had been done. The big fish was spooked and once again turned downstream and out of the swim leaving the rest of the shoal undisturbed and me helpless and frustrated yet again.

Several summers have passed and I have not seen her since, although other anglers have. Still, a new summer is just around the corner and perhaps I will get another chance at the only chub I know of that can make my heart beat fast and set my hands trembling.

PART FIVE

IN THE WAKE OF PREDATORS

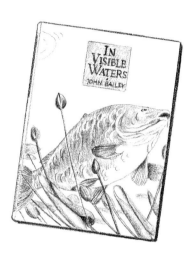

*"When you take a boat from Martham Ferry,
head west and then turn north up Candle
Dyke, you begin to sense another world, and
when you pass the old eel set and the
hunting lodge on the corner and get into the
southern fringes of the Sound, you know
you are really there."*

JOHN BAILEY
In Visible Waters (1984)

Chapter Nineteen

HEYDAYS OF BROADLAND

Piece by piece, the puzzle of the Thurne system had gradually taken shape. The rumours, the facts; the guesses, the confirmations. The blanks, the blind alleys and then finally the fish.

The pointers had been there all along but we had been blind to them. From as early as 1979, the now famous report had appeared in the *Angling Times* of the capture by Robin Stone of a 38lb pike and several other fish over twenty pounds from an undisclosed broad.

This report had set the Broadland pike angling scene buzzing with discussions on which water could produce such an incredible fish, if indeed it was authentic and the accompanying poor quality photograph was nothing if not impressive. With hindsight it seems obvious that only one system could produce such pike. History was repeating itself. The Thurne system, or at least part of it, was back with a vengeance and somewhere in the vastness of those inland seas and waterways, small pockets of large pike had survived the devastation of the prymnesium outbreaks of the late sixties. They had survived and multiplied, undisturbed until one such pocket had been stumbled upon by this lucky angler.

Since the late sixties and the demise of pike fishing on the Thurne broads, pike anglers had often referred to 'The Heyday of Broadland'. Little did they know that as the 1980's dawned, that heyday was about to be surpassed - dramatically.

Prior to 1968, only four 35lb plus pike had been recorded from the Thurne broads.

Arthur Jackson's 35½ pounder from Heigham Sounds in 1948, Reg Pownall's 35 pounder from Martham Broad in 1961, Frank Wright's 35 pounder from Horsey Mere in 1967 and of course, Peter Hancock's 40 pounder, also from Horsey Mere in 1967. This number of 35lb plus fish would be equalled almost within the first year of this new 'heyday'!

Shortly after this first report, another tiny piece appeared, this time in the *Eastern Daily Press*, entitled '28lb pike was dead', it actually mentioned Somerton by name, a place that in only a matter of months would become synonymous with monster pike. But for now, a few tentative trips following up the lead yielded only the inevitable jacks and as other waters were producing large pike, they could not be ignored for less certain waters.

If only we had known what lurked beneath the crystal clear waters of the upper Thurne, in amongst the Marestail and Starwort. Pike almost beyond our wildest dreams. Fish with crocodile heads, in excess of four feet long and some larger than any English pike angler had ever set hooks into before.

Other pointers began to appear in the local and angling press during 1981 and 1982 in the shape of fantastic captures of large pike, but were misleading to say the least. Derrick Amies and James Forte were two of the first anglers to be successful around the Somerton area with pike to 36lbs. Along with Paul Coull and John Tipple, who caught pike to 33lbs, they reported their captures as from Hickling broad; an understandable course of action in the circumstances, although 'the Thurne system' would probably have been misleading enough.

145

In July 1982, the spotlight was once again to fall on the Thurne at Somerton. A report in the *Eastern Evening News* of 14th July told the story of a young holiday angler and his remarkable capture of a colossal 37lb pike on a hot summer's day.

It didn't take long for us to realise that our earlier leads concerning Somerton were completely accurate. It later transpired that the Coull and Tipple fish had been weighed and photographed at Somerton, confirming our own findings after the event.

Rumours, later confirmed, also began to filter through to us that one very shy, retiring but very able and experienced angler, Bill Florey, had also enjoyed incredible success around the head waters of the Thurne. Over a period spanning only two seasons he had captured eight pike in excess of thirty pounds, the largest at 37lbs, innumerable twenty pounders, including a catch of eight in one day and his best season, his last there when he totalled fifty twenty pounders. This total had reached forty nine as the rumours began to leak out. Other anglers including our small band, had begun to fish the system hard and he only returned to catch one further twenty, to bring his total for one season to fifty. A tally that many pike anglers will not realise in two lifetimes.

Unbeknown to our small group, other local anglers had also been following the leads and some appeared on the scene around the same time. Anglers such as Dave Plummer, Paul Belston, Roger Westgate and John Watson, and slowly as the months passed by, the word inevitably leaked out and soon, many well known faces were to be seen along the Thurne.

Prior to these events, I wrote an article in the April '81 issue of *Coarse Fisherman* that uncannily predicted some of the events that were to occur later on the Thurne system. The 'hero' of the piece was based upon two real anglers; Bill Florey and Dennis Pye. It was a fictional tale based on isolated facts and I did not connect the tale and the events that followed on the Thurne concerning Bill, until pointed out by an observant Jim Bigden as we fished a local carp lake many years later. The article was entitled *'The Grebe'*

Chapter Twenty

THE GREBE

Bill was of the old school of pike anglers. Born and bred in Norfolk he had carried out his apprenticeship during the halcyon days of Hickling, Horsey and Heigham Sounds. He was no stranger to twenty pound pike, having lost count of the number he had taken over that weight. His two largest pike weighed 31lbs and 33lbs and now stared balefully down from the wall of this angling study. The two glass cases, mounted on the same wall over the fireplace, were divided by a gap of over four feet. This gap, maintained Bill, was reserved for the English record, rod caught pike, which he would one day capture, for this was his burning ambition and his sole objective in life.

But since the prymnesium disasters of 1967 and the following summers, Bill was a broken man. His world had vanished literally overnight. That morning as he had rowed his boat out from the staithe at Hickling was one he would never forget. The still air had been laden with the stench of rotting fish clogging the reedbeds and he had almost decided to end his angling career there and then. But he had carried on in the knowledge that the gap over the fireplace

148

would never be filled if he could not come to terms with his catastrophic loss.

And so, turning over a new leaf in his angling life, he set out in search of a water that would produce a record pike of over 40 pounds.

He scoured maps, visited waters, and read and re-read old angling books and magazines, slowly whittling out the waters in Broadland until he had a short list from where he thought his quest might end.

One night in his study, well past the bewitching hour, he happened across an item in an old *Creel* magazine that was to bring one location sharply into focus and soaring to the top of his short list. The capture in 1901 of a pike of 42 pounds! The location was a large exposed broad not far from his Norfolk home. He knew of other large pike of over 30lbs from the broad and its adjoining river system and so decided to channel all his efforts onto this one water until that gap over the fireplace had been filled or his time ran out.

It was the middle of March and the weather was milder. Bill had now fished the broad for almost two complete piking seasons but had little to show for his intensive efforts. His largest pike had weighed a little under 15lbs and Bill was somewhat despondent. The problem of location on such a large broad was indeed daunting but one incident had encouraged him to return. During the previous close season he had seen a truly enormous female pike spawning with her attendant smaller males. It would have put his two glass-cased friends to shame.

Today had been the last session he could fish before the season closed and as he packed away his tackle, he reflected on previous seasons and wondered if the next would be any more productive. He rowed slowly back to shore and was deep in thought when a commotion in front of the boat shattered his day dreams.

Upon turning, he could see a young great creasted

grebe obviously in distress, thrashing around in ever decreasing circles. Bill had always regarded grebes as his friends. They had often lead him to shoals of bait fish in the past, and ultimately to pike. He decided to help the unfortunate creature.

The boat drifted towards the bird and Bill gently covered it with his landing net. The deep meshes encompassed it easily and once aboard it was apparent that the grebe was badly injured. It had probably been hit by a speed boat as one leg and one wing were obviously broken. Bill thought back to the old days when he had started piking with old Ben. Motor boats had been few and far between in those days and had not often fouled the tranquility of Broadland with their noise and filth. This type of thing certainly would not have happened then.

He took the bird home and set its leg and wing to the best of his ability. Surprisingly it became quite tame in the months that it shared Bill's small cottage but finally, the time came for it to be released and Bill felt a tinge of loneliness as he drove his trusty motor-bike and side car to the broad, with the grebe secure in his wicker basket. It seemed reluctant to regain its freedom and stayed close to the staithe for a while. Bill silently hoped that it would return but eventually, testing its mended limbs, it headed out into the wind. Bill turned his back on the broad and headed home to an empty cottage.

Summer came and went and soon Bill was preparing his pike tackle for the coming winter. He had almost forgotten the grebe now, but with the first pike session approaching, he decided to pack his binoculars in the hope that he might renew acquaintances.

The first day of October and Bill knew that the chance of a really big pike was very slim. Still, after six months without wetting a line except to catch his livebait, he could restrain himself no longer.

He reached the broad well before dawn and was soon heading out slowly against a stiff breeze with strong, steady pulls on the oars. The bows cut cleanly through the waves as he headed out to his chosen swim where he knew the bream fishers had made impressive catches during the summer months. They had observed large pike in the same area and on occasion, tackle had been smashed as bream of over two pounds were taken from the hook by ravenous pike.

Bill quietly anchored and lowered the livebait, a bream of similiar size, into the murky water. He paid off line from the large centrepin as the bait steadily began to swim upwind, away from the boat.

He had been watching his float intently for several hours without result when, much to his surprise, an old friend popped up between it and him. It was the grebe, recognised by its slightly deformed wing. The bird came very close to the boat and seemed to recognise Bill but finally moved off to an area of deeper water about seventy-five yards to his left. He watched it through binoculars, fascinated as it dived and surfaced making a considerable commotion. Bill had a strange compulsion to follow the bird and had decided on a move on in any case. He soon had the boat positioned over the area and once again paid off line from the centrepin as the bream swam off.

It certainly had not swam off that fast before, thought Bill. Could it be a take already?

The line, flowing though his palm, slowed as his fingers tightened over it. Something powerful kept the line moving and Bill's heart beat a little faster. The float submerged and the seconds ticked by. The line jerked to a stop and Bill wound down to the fish, hoping it had not dropped the large bait. Feeling the weight of the pike he bent the hefty split cane rod into its battle curve and with an alarming thud, the rod jerked in the direction of the fish as it moved off.

The initial action was exciting but soon over and the remainder of the fight was uneventful as can often be the case with Broadland pike. Bill weighed it in his landing net at 26½lbs, the first fish of that weight he had caught for a long time. He was pleased but he had been there before. It was not what he had set his sights on but nevertheless, a step in the right direction.

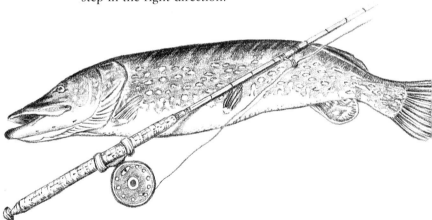

The other sessions on the broad that season followed a similiar pattern. It seemed as if the grebe knew of Bill's quest and was guiding him to those areas on the vast broad frequented by the larger pike in repayment of his kindness. As the season progressed and autumn turned to winter, Bill's tally of big twenties steadily rose. He became the talk of the angling world, first locally, and then nationally, as word inevitably leaked out. He even bettered his largest pike, but stood by the standard he had set himself and returned it to the broad. He was sure the fish he had observed was even larger.

The season moved towards its close and Bill realised that the big females would now be at their largest. It was the second weekend in March and Bill once again found himself on the Broad, scanning its surface for the grebe. It didn't usually take long to locate and if he couldn't then the grebe would find him. Today was no exception and Bill was soon following the grebe as it swam in the direction of a large shallow bay known to Bill as the 'Back Bay'. It was an area he had never even considered.

On entering the bay, the grebe, seemed somewhat apprehensive, but finally headed in until it had almost reached the shore where a tangle of roots and bushes cascaded from the bank into the water.

Bill anchored his boat about forty feet from the grebe and scanned the surface near the roots and bushes with his binoculars. All was very still. Or was it? Did the water 'hump' just then? He blinked and looked again. A small swirl disturbed the surface. There was definitely a fish there, but how big was it?

As if in answer an enormous back heaved out of the water followed by the top of a gigantic tail that formed oily ripples until the surface stilled once again. He instinctively knew that this was the large female he had observed spawning before, and here she was again after acting out that same ritual.

With shaking hands he rigged up his trace with a large bream livebait as the grebe continued to circle the area. Bill had begun to swing the bait out but the cast was never completed, for as he glanced in the direction of the grebe, it seemed to lift in the water. With eyes bulging, neck outstretched and beak snapping, it screeched in agony and then was gone. A stream of bubbles broke the surface and tiny feathers spun round on tiny eddies where the bird had been, and then all was very quiet and very still.

He stared aghast at the water long after the last ripple had died away, unable to believe the drama he had witnessed. Nevertheless, he fished on thoughout the day and long into darkness. But in vain. It seemed that another season in search of a record pike had slipped furtively by.

If anything, the incident with the grebe had confirmed Bill's theories and encouraged him. He was sad at the demise of his friend but by the end of yet another season he was once again struggling. His largest pike had tipped the scales at a little under 15lbs.

Chapter Twenty One

MEMORABLE PIKE

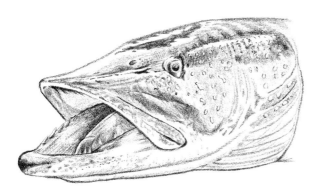

After the fictional interlude of *The Grebe*, we return to reality. Basing our Thurne campaign on confirmed facts, it was decided that our four man team of Dave Humphries, Martyn Page, Charles Beane and myself would concentrate on this river and it's ajoining broads during the coming pike season of 1982/83.

Plans were laid and theories expounded. We were certain that we were now in the right area but after several sessions in the Autumn of 1982 none of our team had connected with any of the larger fish. We had caught pike, mostly jacks and some fish just scraping into double figures but the leviathans were conspicuous by their absence.

Then, very early in 1983, after a brief relapse onto easier waters, catching a number of pike to over 20lbs, we returned and finally connected with some Thurne lunkers.

A Sunday in early January and a cool, overcast day dawned with a moderate westerly rustling the reeds over Broadland, rippling the khaki green surface of the slowly moving river.

I fished from my own boat and Charles, a short distance upstream, in his. Martyn and Dave fished together, just out of sight around the next curve in the river.

The River Thurne at Somerton.

Charles had the first sign of action, a dropped take even as I silently manouvered my boat into position tight alongside the reeds. But I did not have to wait long, once settled. Within five minutes I was playing a spirited 7lber that had taken a fancy to my float paternostered livebait in midstream.

By 9.10am, three other small pike, all under five pounds, had put in an appearance but it seemed that, as far as large pike were concerned, once again my swim was barren. I considered a move but a deep seated, nagging doubt insisted against it and I changed the positions of the baits instead.

My boat was tied to the reeds at the downstream corner of a small bay in the river bank. I recast one bait upstream, and upwind and it landed at the other corner, close to the reeds. I reeled down tightly to the sunken float paternoster, pushing in the multipliers' ratchet and releasing the spool button. The ratchet clicked repeatedly as I replaced the rod across the boat ensuring a very tight line to the bait. In the event of a pike taking line, the ratchet would sound. If the fish moved towards me the line would slacken at the rod tip. I sat back to await events, pulling the lines occasionally to keep the baits lively.

9.40am, thirty minutes without a run even from a microlight jack and I was again thinking of a move when the line fell slack. I had been watching the rod tip, it's movements increasingly violent as the bait became agitated, then ceasing as it had been engulfed. It could mean only one thing and I reeled down, feeling the resistance before setting the hooks. The fish fought all over the swim, more like a fifteen pounder than the 20lbs plus that I estimated as she neared the surface, before diving off under the boat. But there were no poles or anchor cables to snag and I regained the line and managed to guide her into the net at the first attempt.

The hooks that had been in the scissors, came out as the fish thrashed in the net but it was too late now and I hoisted it onto the scales with the use of an oar to record my largest pike at that time of 27lbs 9ozs.

Charles, seeing the fish going 'up on the oar' came over to investigate and congratulate, then sped off downstream to inform Dave and Martyn of the news. While he was away, casts to the same area produced pike of 11lbs 1oz and 6lbs before Charles returned to say that Dave had also struck gold and taken a large concorde-nosed pike of 25lbs 5ozs and that he would meet half way to take photographs.

What an incredible day. Our determination to succeed had paid off and we had discovered the Thurne pike with a bang.

After measuring and photographing the two leviathans, we returned them to their weedy domain and continued fishing until we could no longer see our way back but it seemed that the Thurne had given up more than it's share of treasures for one day and we had no other runs.

The next weekend we set out onto the water with great expectations but, as is often the case in angling, it turned out to be a complete anti-climax. Only two small pike appeared and it almost seemed as if we were back to square one, much to our disappointment after covering a great deal of water.

The following weekend and we were back once again, determined not to be beaten so easily. Fortunately, the pendulum was about to swing once again, this time in our favour.

The dawn of another overcast and cold Saturday and January was drawing to a close. Martyn and I launched my boat into the dyke, turning right at the main river and headed the boat towards Somerton between the reed fringed banks with the wind at our backs.

The engine was switched off long before we reached the area we intended to fish and I rowed quietly toward the swim we had selected, slightly down from the 'bay' where I had earlier taken the 27 pounder. The first bait was cast at 7.55am and the others followed shortly. The ratchets engaged on the multipliers, we eagerly anticipated the first 'run music' of the morning. We didn't have long to wait.

At 8.05am, after only ten minutes in the swim and the ratchet to my left hand rod, a sunken float paternostered roach in midstream, gave a short, sharp 'zizz' and then fell silent. It was a definite take, I remarked to Martyn, and picked up the rod with the usual anticipation of a run on the Thurne. It could be two pounds, it could be forty-two pounds. Waters are few and far between that give you the shakes even as a take develops!

The bait was small and the hooks were soon struck into the pike whatever its size, but there was no give at all in the rod. A small pike is usually pulled through the water with the power of the strike. This time the rod arched violently in the direction of this immoveable, unseen force and the clutch gave line momentarily. After this initial shock, I seemed to briefly gain control but the fish had probably swum at an angle, almost in towards the boat. When under full pressure from the straining rod once again, the fish seemed to realise that all was not well and decided to do something about it.

It headed off in an uncontrollable circuit of the boat, running deep but slowly, tangling other lines in its wake and setting other ratchets screaming until finally surfacing roughly in the same area where the bait had been originally taken. Nervously, I mentioned that we might need the net for this one and for the first time during the battle, I could see the fish clearly and began to fully appreciate its true size, beginning to shake as I did so. After much tooing and froing, just out of netting range she finally began to tire and slowly edged towards, and then over the net cord, gills flaring in a last vain thrash. But the net had already been expertly lifted by Martyn and we secured it to the rowlock while the decks were quickly cleared to receive our guest.

She looked incredibly long, laying on the carpeting in the well of my small punt, nose in one corner and tail almost up over the seat.

"It seems to go on forever!" exaggerated Martyn and I bit the line through, losing the float, in an effort to make the unhooking as fast and clean as possible. It was no easy matter trying to prise those massive jaws apart to remove the trebles but they were de-barbed and only just inside, so it took only a matter of seconds before the weigh sling was full to overflowing.

We had our doubts from the start that the thirty-two pound 'Avon' scales would be adequate and with due ceremony, they were bumped to the limit. On Martyn's forty-four pound scales, a weight of 32lbs 9ozs was recorded after the sling had been subtracted and I felt somewhat numb, an aim achieved, a dream reality and the events of the morning taking on a dreamlike quality as they finally sunk in.

The dimensions were to prove almost as big a shock as catching that first thirty pounder. $47\frac{1}{2}$ inches with a girth of $23\frac{1}{4}$ inches. Hancocks forty pounder had been exactly the same length but with almost three more inches on the

32lbs 9ozs; an aim achieved, a dream reality.

girth and much fatter all along those mottled flanks of
almost four feet long. We wondered at the potential of my
fish and tried to guess the maximum weight it had attained
or would achieve in its life time. She almost certainly had
made 35lbs plus at sometime, perhaps during February or
March, ripe with spawn, or at the tail end of last summer,
with a belly full of Thurne bream.

To these questions, we shall never know the answers
but its always interesting to surmise. Maybe the next time
she is captured, she will have the girth of Hancock's fish as
well as the length, if the inevitable prymnesium outbreaks
of the following summers do not claim her first.

Chapter Twenty Two

A HECTIC HALF HOUR

Some waters are very special; of that there is little doubt. It is an acknowledged fact amongst many true anglers that a small, select number of waters have that certain something that sets them apart from their peers.

They may be known nationally, such as Redmire Pool and Loch Lomond, or they may be known on a regional basis by the local anglers that fish them, regarded in the same esteem by those fortunate to be attuned to their distinctiveness.

A chalk stream or a carp pool, a Norfolk broad or a Scottish loch; this special quality knows no boundaries. Aura or charisma, call it what you will, it is the water that holds the mystery and the mystery that, like a magnet, draws the angler irresistibly to it, with its history, beauty and a promise of the fish of dreams.

One such water for me is Horsey Mere; 'A broad in all but name', as Peter Collins described it in his 1967 guide *Fishing the Norfolk Broads.* Only two years later, this jewel in the Thurne crown was to suffer the total devastation that is prymnesium. But it had bounced back from death before.

The sand dunes of the east coast are easily seen from Horsey Mere and on most days, the waves of the North Sea can be heard crashing onto the shore. In February,

1938, the sea broke through the sand hills that form this costal defence and opened up a breach of half a mile. The combined effect of gale force, north-west winds and high tides on the full moon, flooded an area covering 7500 acres. Almost all the Thurne catchment area was effected and all freshwater fish in Horsey Mere were killed with the exception of eels.

The land was covered with sea water for over three months, the pumps and windmills working around the clock, once the breach had been secured, to restore the land. But the destruction was complete. Not only fish suffered, the most obvious victims, but most of the other forms of wildlife were devastated, directly or indirectly.

Vegetation was eradicated; earthworms wiped out and the moles and birdlife that depended upon them, also tragically effected. The total lack of mice and rats forced the birds of prey to leave; in fact all the wildlife of the area suffered to a lesser or greater extent, from the majestic Marsh Harrier to the humble worm.

It took a very long while for Horsey to return to normality and for its water to be once again fresh. Every pike in Hickling, Horsey and Heigham Sounds had been killed and the task of restoring the areas pike fishing was taken on by one man; Jim Vincent.

During the war years of 1939-1945, he moved a great many pike, mainly from Ranworth Broad, into the Thurne system, thereby assuring the future of pike fishing in the area and the heydays that were to follow. On one such restocking trip, he and an associate transferred 49 pike totalling 276lbs using barbless hooks to avoid damaging the pike! It is interesting to speculate that if the actions of Jim Vincent did have a profound effect on the area with his injection of Bure-caught pike, then the large and big-headed Thurne pike, so famous throughout the angling world, are a product of the system and its waters and not an evolutionary trait as has sometimes been suggested. I am sure that any pike, wherever it might be moved from, would soon adapt and take full advantage of the uniqueness of the Thurne system to reach its full potential.

The Norfolk reed is all around, the skyline broken only by the occasional windmill and copse. The marsh harrier, swooping low over the reed beds in search of prey, epitomises the wild beauty that is Horsey Mere. But it is not only this beauty that is so attractive. A long history of gigantic pike, that in Norfolk is second to none, is obviously the main factor that lures the pikemen.

Unfortunately, Horsey's track record in more recent years has been none too impressive. Since 1969, a succession of further prymnesium outbreaks have consolidated the initial destruction. Each time the pike population has made some sort of recovery, another outbreak is confirmed that sets the healing process back once again.

Pre-prymnesium, in the closing six weeks of 1967, it was a very different story and Horsey was definitely *the* place to be. Hancock's forty pounder is obviously the fish most remembered from this period, but it did not end there. Other very knowledgeable anglers were fishing the mere for those six weeks and their tally of twenty and thirty pound pike from one water, in so short a period of time, was phenomenal.

Spencer's '34'

34lbs to Len Spencer, 32lbs 12ozs, 31lbs and three others over twenty pounds to Frank Wright, 31lbs to David Hazard, 29lbs and 27lbs to an unknown angler, 28½lbs to Albert Wright, 28lbs to Peter Nisbit, 27lbs to Edward Vincent, 25lbs to Colin Dyson and five fish over twenty pounds to Dennis Pye, plus other fish over twenty pounds that in such company, hardly warranted a mention. It is interesting to speculate on the number and sizes of pike in Horsey at that time. Was the largest fish (i.e. Hancock's) caught?

Hancock's '40'

It was with the memory of this past glory that interest in Horsey was rekindled in the early eighties for a small number of seasoned Norfolk pikemen new to the Thurne. They reasoned that the potential of such a water is *always* present to produce an exceptional fish, but times had changed - dramatically. Pike were contacted, mostly jacks with the occassional larger fish but twenties and thirties were now extremly rare. As the seasons passed, with subsequent outbreaks of prymnesium, the numbers of pike of all sizes continued to dwindle; but for just one day during that period, I was extremely fortunate.

Over the winter evenings, I had been reading up on the Thurne system and in particular, on Horsey and its illustrious past. Articles in old magazines, sections in out of print angling books, guides to Broadland fishing and maps of the area. Before the short season on Horsey had opened that year, I already had a feeling for the water. Strangely that feeling seemed, again and again, to focus my attention on one small bay in particular as I read and re-read through the stories, photographs and maps.

And so, as I headed my boat out against a gentle ripple into the vastness of Horsey on that cool and overcast March dawn, there was no question in my mind about where to fish. This strange instinct had guided me there days before.

There seemed little need to hurry. Other boats were already positioned including those of my friends Martyn Page and Dave and Gary Humphries but none were close to my intended swim.

The breeze blew gently into the bay rippling the surface as I positioned the boat directly opposite the left hand corner where it meets the main broad. I cast my deadbaits into the coloured water and settled comfortably onto the cushion to await events with the first cup of tea of the day. (Always the best one.)

After about forty minutes in the swim, I thought I noticed the float to the herring rod give a sharp dip. It was one of those occasions when you almost wonder if you have imagined the occurance, after all, isn't it possible to stare a float into invisibility? I reeled in after a short while as nothing further had materialised and noted the lack of weed here. The bait was unmarked and it was possible that a fish had swum onto the line.

Wildlife is welcome distraction whilst fishing and I always note down any interesting sightings in my angling diary. At 8.12am, a kingfisher flashed past and I wondered if it would bring me luck. I didn't wonder for long. It heralded a run that followed after ten minutes, my assumption about the first sign of action, probably correct.

I reeled and reeled, the fish running fast in towards me, the rod finally curving over as I made contact but only very briefly, the bait returning with tiny pin-prick holes across it and I prayed it was a jack but realised I was shaking! This *was* Horsey.

No other signs of life by 9am and so I up-anchored quietly and drifted into the bay itself, that strange feeling still strong and feeding my confidence. Something was going to happen, I just knew it!

Not bothering to sit down in the boat or get comfortable, I checked that the decks were clear and ready for action. It took fifteen minutes for the herring float to sail away, the strike making the boat swing round. It was obviously a good fish and the first glimpse through the murky water confirmed this. I was therefore understandably concerned when, after initially securing the fish at the first attempt, it promptly turned around and leapt clear of the net! Playing the fish back again, I made sure that didn't happen again.

A second rod was very quickly reeled in and cast to the position of the first run while my guest waited in the landing net. The timing of the next run was perfect. I had just weighed and sacked the first fish, ready for photography and the re-cast rod was away. After a fairly short tussle, with no exciting escapes this time, another hefty pike was soon secure in the landing net, hung over the rowlock.

The same procedure was followed once again as I quickly re-cast the last baited rod back into what was fast becoming quite a 'hotspot'. I was just about to lift the second fish out in the landing net and 'zizz', the re-cast rod was away again!

One pike in a sack, one in the landing net, (quickly re-attached to the rowlock), and yet another run. Things were getting somewhat hectic and this time I realised I had quite a problem on my hands having to net this latest pike

A hectic half-hour.

with one already filling the landing net!

As it transpired, the netting of the third fish proved less of a problem than I had anticipated. The previous pike thankfully stayed well down in the deep mesh and the other fish joined it easily on the first try as I sunk the net only briefly, another long fish sliding painfully slowly over the net cord. The two fish were unhooked in turn without problems, the de-barbed trebles always a great asset, the second fish waiting in the net as I lifted out the first.

From the time of the first run at 9.15am to the netting of the third fish, less than half an hour had elapsed but what a hectic half hour. Only anglers can truely appreciate the rare, intense periods of action packed minutes in such contrast to the hours and hours of long inactivity.

'Bag' shots are thankfully a thing of the past in today's enlightened big fish scene. It is rare to keep more than one fish sacked for photography. In this case, I had little choice, the runs coming in such quick succession, the first resulting in a 21lbs 11oz fish, the second a 20lbs 2oz and the third, 21lbs exactly, all such beautiful fish with a turquoise hue so characteristic of Horsey pike. Perhaps it would have been more agreeable to savour the action, spread out over the session. Still, I did have three more doubles to 17lbs throughout the day and I certainly wouldn't have missed such excitement!

Chapter Twenty Three

THURNE EPILOGUE

S ummer on the broads, with the vast armada of holiday craft and their attendant 'crash course cruiser captains'; it is the place I least like to be. As the leaves turn to browns and golds, the air cools and winter inevitably approaches, the broadland scene changes . The boat traffic declines rapidly, then dies, becoming almost negligible. The reeds fade from their bright summer green to the brittle beige of winter. Cold winds cut across the flat Norfolk landscape and the herons retreat to the boatyards, following the nervous roach shoals.

The pike fisherman on broadland, afloat as always, will see other boats but in all probability, the majority will be other pike fishermen, on the water for the same reason. But even these boats are fewer nowadays on the Thurne system. The number of pike has declined dramatically since the heady days of the early eighties when rediscovered by a small band of intrepid locals. This has in part been due to the persistent outbreaks of prymnesium most summers, a problem that Anglian Water seems powerless against. Much has been written and said on the subject, the causes are well known and something is also known about the solution, but I fear it is one problem that we will have to live with in Norfolk for many years to come.

Pike boats moored on the Thurne.

The other main reason for the decline in the Thurne pike stocks is pike angling itself, some of it very bad pike angling. Fish killed for trophies, handled carelessly, a take left too long, a line breakage on the strike, a bad paternoster rig inducing a bite off, a trace snapped in heavy weed and generally the heavy angling pressure that pursued them even in the summer months when fish were retained and died after fighting hard in the heat of summer, with prymnesium still present.

The first 'heyday' of Hancock, Jackson, Pownall, Wright and Pye had come and gone, departing almost overnight with the smell of rotting fish choking the summer reedbeds. Some Norfolk anglers hung up their rods in 1969 with broken hearts.

The second 'heyday' passed somewhat less dramatically, after the Thurne pike had been rediscovered for a second time in recent history. This time the sizes of the largest pike had overshadowed the captures of the sixties but nothing is forever in the world of angling and now, a day on the Thurne is as if fishing after the gold rush.

The seclusion, alone in a boat in a wild, windswept

environment is still attractive and I enjoy fishing these places even without catching vast numbers of fish but that bonus of a shaking hand as the float slides, then dips away is perhaps gone until another ten or twelve years have slipped by.

The Thurne system however, always surprizes with its resiliance, bouncing back after every prymnesium outbreak. The truly large pike which regained the Thurne's reputation in the early eighties are now non-exsistent save for perhaps the odd monster hidden and secluded in sanctuary. Smaller fish to the high twenties are still reported each season particularly from the upper Thurne but these press reports are often very misleading. For instance, one pike known as 'the E pike', due to a noticeable marking on its left flank, was captured seven times during one winter ranging from 27lbs 12ozs to 29lbs 3ozs and was reported in the angling press almost as many times. It looks great from a distance, big pike coming out almost every weekend but when you realise that this sport revolves around a very small number of big pike, the picture is very different and not quite so rosy.

Charles Beane in action.

A Thurne 'thirty' is returned.

Martyn Page with a 30lbs 2oz fish.

Contrary to popular belief, even in the early eighties, twenties and thirties did not come out every weekend. It was always a hard water unless you were lucky enough to be sitting on top of a pack of feeding fish. Now twenties are not common and thirties almost unheard of. But I am glad to have been there and part of it in some small way. Perhaps the new generation of pike anglers will talk of it as we do of the pike caught during the sixties. Perhaps one day we will even see the third coming of the unique pike fishing on the Thurne system.

PART SIX
PASTURES NEW

"The day was roasting hot and I shall never forget the sight of a vast shoal of carp, some perfect monsters, sunning themselves at their lordly ease just under the surface."

"No account of battles with big carp and barbel would be complete without some reference to their relatives in the East, the best known of which is the mighty mahseer."

'BB'
The Fisherman's Bedside Book (1945)

Chapter Twenty Four

TOWERTREE POOL

Towertree Pool was simply quite beautiful. I fell under its spell from the very first evening I walked the secluded banks and gazed into the shallow, clear waters at the great carp that hung almost motionless out towards its centre, like the illustrations from a 'BB' book.

It's beauty was not that of the well kept and manicured club water, with its stagings and trimmed branches, but of the wild and overgrown neglect of a forgotten estate lake. Over the years, the pool had gradually silted and this process, along with recent long hot summers, had reduced the overall depth to two and three feet, the deepest areas perhaps only four feet. Much of the bottom was of soft silt and light weed but some areas, especially those where the carp were seen to feed, were of a harder sandier nature.

Fishing was only allowed from the north bank. The main area of this bank was devoid of any cover at all, save for a few thistles. It made stalking carp, or simply staying out of view, impossible and I knew that coming to terms with this lake would be no easy matter.

The far bank, in contrast, was simply an impenetrable jungle. I would have loved to fish from its all-concealing branches but luckily, the carp did seem to favour this north side of the lake; I would have to overcome the lack of cover.

A plan of action evolved slowly as I began to get a feel for this magnificent water and its carp. Baits were important but I would give them more thought as I observed the movements and habits of the lake's inhabitants using binoculars and polaroids and watching for movement patterns and intense feeding activity.

Towertree was something of an enigma. A water almost lost in time, it had not seen the carp revolution and I doubted that the carp knew a paste bait let alone a boilie. In any case, it seemed to go totally against the grain to fish such a water using modern methods and baits. A lake that should be fished with cane Mk. IVs, claw bail arm Mitchells, Heron bite alarms and the rustle of silver paper at the butt ring.

I decided to experiment intially with naturals such as maggots and worms but also to introduce a small amount of particles at the end of each day that I fished, in the hope that as the weeks passed they would eventually be accepted as part of the natural food supply.

It was now August and Britain, along with the carp of Towertree, basked in the hottest summer since 1976. Even the shallowest margins of the lake were frequented by the carp. With their dorsals and backs breaking the surface, they would cruise through or feed briefly disturbing great clouds of mustard coloured silt into fantastic, changing shapes and then quickly moving on, they would pause elsewhere, never feeding for any great length of time in these tropical conditions.

Maggots seemed the first logical choice of bait, as close perhaps as I could attain to the carp's natural diet. I baited several of the most favoured areas with live and dead maggots, the latter acting I hoped, as a beacon whist the live maggots soon wriggled into the silt and out of sight.

Four maggots, made bouyant with a small piece of foam, completed the light, link-ledger rig, fished at two inches off the bottom. It looked so good it just had to work. And so it did.

Within two hours of the first session, the line streaked out and I hit into something that immediately began to kite to the right along the shallow margin. It didn't feel at all weighty and I hoped for a small carp but my fears were soon confirmed. The culprit was a bream. One of the small shoal of large bream known to inhabit the lake, it took the scales down to 8lbs 12ozs. Still at least it proved the effectiveness of the rig in making my hookbait prominent and highly visible in amongst the multitude of free offerings.

Encouraged, I fished all the harder but the carp were not so easily fooled.

During the following two sessions, I tried many other baits and every trick in the book to tempt the carp that were much in evidence close to the swims I fished. At times they bubbled or bow-waved, smoke-screened and even leaped, mocking me as they hit into my lines, giving me frequent heart palpitations. But as for carp runs, they were only a dream, and yet I had a feeling that given time, the dream would become reality. It was time to see if the particles would work.

Along a short length of the north bank, where there were a few trees, the branches always shaded the water. Several carp favoured this brief patrol route, sometimes cruising but often bubbling. I would try here first with the particles on my next session.

I could hardly wait as the days dragged slowly by but the allotted day finally arrived. Late August now and although it would not be light until 5am, I was up and ready at 2.30am, the pool and its carp gradually becoming an obsession.

There were no stars or moon to reflect on the surface. The night seemed pitch black as I walked silently to the water, my eyes gradually becoming accustomed to the lack of light as I blended with the shadows and became part of the night. The roosting birdlife had not been disturbed; I hoped the carp were just as unaware.

I cast the first bait out into the darkness at 3.40am, as close as possible to the overhanging branches, dreading the sound of the lead in the leaves that thankfully did not come. Only two pouchfuls of bait into the swim so as not to disturb any carp in residence and not to outnumber my two tiny hookbaits lost in the debris and confusion of the lake bed.

The night was muggy; no need of the Barbour. The thin cloud cover had held in the heat of yesterday and the lake's surface was calm apart from occasional gusts that were fresh in my face. All was quiet, still and dark. Even the coots slept and there was no sign of bow-wave or swirl to reflect upon the dark pool.

Less than an hour had passed and there was just the faintest hint of dawn in the sky. The first cup of tea had just been poured and was destined to be wasted. I was away on the right-hand rod. It was not a roaring, runaway bite, as often carp runs are, but a twitching, confident lift, gradually getting faster as the fish realised something was amiss. I struck as the handle began to move and pulled hard to coax the carp away from the branches. It didn't need too much persuasion and was soon in open water but fast heading for the other bank and its attendant roots and snags! Drastic measures were called for. I scrabbled about in the half light for a few stones with the rod bucking against my other arm and threw them awkwardly between the snags and the fish. It worked just in time, the fish turning abruptly out into the open water again and I tried to ensure that the rest of the battle would be played out there, side-straining hard if there was any concerted effort to the left or right. There was much tooing and froing at the net, not helped by many early morning bats that repeatedly hit the line in the twilight as I played the fish, netting it finally on the third attempt.

The number six 'Jack Hilton' was securely lodged just inside the left hand side of the mouth and to say I was pleased with my first carp from a new and very hard water, was rather an under-statement and conclusive proof that they were onto my bait. Not the largest carp in Norfolk at 15lbs 12ozs but very welcome indeed and a real battler, it had taken twenty minutes to subdue. Surprising though, that the run had come completely out of the blue. No line lifts or twitches had preceded the action, but they were there nevertheless.

Not the largest carp in Norfolk at 15lbs 12ozs.

The pool had settled down again by 5.30am and it was now fully light, a breeze springing up into my face shortly after. At 5.50am a large area of bubbles erupted in the remaining calm area by the far bank and I was keyed up, expecting further action.

A carp was surely responsible and confirmation soon followed. A broad, purple head and back, topped by a huge fan-like dorsal, porpoised briefly close by, leaving rings that spread and faded slowly. I cast a rod over the area of activity, drew the bait back into it and had liners immediately that teased but did not develop.

In fact activity died down although carp were moving out towards the centre of the lake. Perhaps my casts had disturbed the swim for it was not until around 8.30am that lifts and plucks recommenced on the lines and bubbles began to reappear here and there about the swim.

8.35am and the right hand buzzer sounded, the indicator lifted then stopped. My trembling hand hovered over the rod as the line continued to twitch where it entered the water. Almost without conscious thought, I struck and found solid resistance in the shape of a very confused carp that didn't realise at first that it had been fooled.

Another hard fighter, this carp made the reel handle spin several times but apart from burying itself in the soft weed, I had few problems and soon netted another mirror a fraction lighter than the first and hooked on the very edge of the lower lip.

It rained from 10.25am but I didn't care. It could snow if it liked. I had finally succeeded and packed up at 12 noon after baiting the swim. Mission accomplished, I was a very happy angler wondering what else, if anything, the lake held in store for me.

I couldn't wait to return to the pool and managed to arrange a day that would mean short sessions before and after work. Even more eager than before, I was up at 2am and settled in my swim just an hour later. The weather was again overcast but cool with a moderate south westerly bringing showers with it, some almost torrential.

As soon as it was light enough, the rain now easing off, I watched the lines intently where they curved gently downward to disappear into the surface film. With even a gentle ripple, it was difficult to watch for bubbles or movements, but at 5.40am a carp gave the game away by bow-waving, submarine-like, out of the swim for some unknown reason. Twenty minutes later, as if to prove there were other carp still in the area of my baits, a liner to the left hand rod pulled at the buzzer four times. But as the morning wore on, it appeared my new found confidence was misplaced.

It didn't seem like hours that I had sat so motionless, enjoying the atmosphere of this timeless lake and the birds that lived there. A kestrel had landed only feet away to bathe just out from the debris line, the jays had squabbled in the treetops and the electric-blue and orange blur of the kingfisher had flashed by several times. Five hours had passed so quickly, why didn't a working day conform to these same rules. And another working day would soon be upon me. It was almost 8am and I would have to reel in at 8.30am at the latest. It semed as if today was not to be 'the' day and so, as a last ditch attempt, I reeled in the left hand rod and retackled with a heavier lead, casting to the furthermost extent of my baited area and returned the rod to its rests.

The lines remained motionless. No lifts, or twitches, or plucks or pulls. No sign of fish now for quite some time; the pool seemed devoid of life. Only minutes left before I would have to head for work and I was resigned to defeat.

"Beeeeeep!" Again the run came out of the blue and I was shocked into action. The left hand rod had only been recast perhaps twenty minutes and the line was moving slowly, the buzzer once again sounding out in anger.

The fish hung heavily, close to the branches for a while, undecided on which way to go it seemed. But with gentle persuasion she ran for the middle of the pool, creating a giant bow-wave that calmed the ripple and I let her go, backwinding grudgingly on the old '300' but content to fight it out in the open water. The course of the fight followed much the same pattern as the previous fish and I only had to apply real pressure once, side straining to head off a bull-nosed charge towards the opposite bank. She turned and headed back towards me, gradually approaching the net as I finally gained a first detailed glimpse, if briefly, of an enormous head through the clear water.

I was shocked, I hadn't realised the true size of my adversary and was taken aback as the carp once again bow-waved out for the centre of the lake. Very carefully now, she was coaxed back to the net a beautiful, fin-perfect, if elderly, mirror of 23lbs 13ozs. I *would* be late for work this morning!

Constantly in awe of Towertree, I was beginning to

A beautiful, fin-perfect, if elderly mirror of 23lbs 13ozs.

think that I had finally conquered the pool, my initial success breeding perhaps, unfound confidence. As often happens in angling, the fish were soon to bring me back to earth with a resounding crash in the unwelcome shape of two lost fish.

The line had parted on the first carp and I was at a loss to understand why. The line was new; I hadn't held the carp particularly hard but we had parted company nevertheless. Not with the 'crack' of line going under pressure but more a soft, gradual breakage of line that has been damaged or weakened by abrasion with some sharp underwater object.

I had reeled fast, hoping that the carp had turned and ran in towards me, but deep down, I knew the reason for the straightness of the rod, the limpness of the line and the hollow, empty feeling of despair after so many fruitless hours of long and patient vigil.

But it does no good to rant and rave. I'm not one to turn the air blue or throw the rod about as some anglers do. Best to be philosophical about such disasters, learn from them and accept that its all in the game. A few fish, especially the more powerful species, such as carp and barbel, will sometimes win a battle, particularly if hooked in confined or snaggy swims.

The second carp had simply come unbuttoned after a frantic fight lasting over ten minutes that must have gradually loosened a feeble hook-hold. The head of the carp was almost at the net cord when hook and tackle catapulted upward, the hook-hold finally giving out. The carp, a dark shadow against the silt, lay just out of netting range and I lunged at it pointlessly, I don't know why. It turned slowly and distainfully, gliding back out into the lake leaving me once again with that hollow, empty feeling.

I consoled myself that the carp was not one of the larger inhabitants of the pool. At least they were still accepting my bait but I hoped desperately to shake off this

jinx with a landing net wet once again in earnest.

Negative thoughts crowded in upon me as the next session at Towertree approached. Would there be more lost fish? Where was I going wrong? Or was it simply bad luck, two lost fish convincing me that I would fail? I did have confidence in my tackle, my bait had caught and it was the swim that was awkward and the carp, or some of them, that were unco-operative and inconsiderate. I would just have to persevere.

But even the next session started off badly. The alarm failed to go off and I didn't get up until just before 3am. It seemed essential to be set-up and fishing well before dawn, giving the carp no hint of my arrival, but I still had plenty of time before then.

I looked out over the pool for quite some time in the clear, cold stillness of the predawn, the plough hanging overhead, its stars this time reflected, floating on a shadowed sheet of shimmering glass. A carp crashed out of the swim as I watched, disturbing the stars. A beautiful welcome, it broke the spell and, I hoped, my jinx.

Flicking out five or six pouches of bait this time, I cast out the two rods with difficulty in the darkness. Once again I felt confident, lost in the beauty of the pool at dawn and a strange thought occured. I was sure that I would come and sit and fish even if I could see into the future and read 'blank' on the pages of my diary. Being here at the best part of the day was reward enough and I remembered I was not the first to appreciate that there is more to fishing than just catching fish.

The dawn came and went and the pool gradually began to awaken to the new day. The kingfisher flew past me just before 6.30am and a carp boiled in the swim leaving an untidy collection of bubbles to add to the flotsam and jetsam of a summer's surface debris.

The lines at the rod tips, still for so long, began to come to life with their attached tiny feathers and strands of weed, twitching and lifting as some unseen, scaled bodies rubbed and scraped against them out in the pool.

The line to the left hand rod twitched, lifted and remained tight, the buzzer sounding, the indicator rising slowly but surely. I struck into nothing realising that a carp must have caught the line securely on a fin or across its back but I saw no sign of it having been alarmed, even in the shallow water.

Almost two hours had passed and carp again began to fizz and froth the surface above my baits, finally picking up one of them and this time charging off, making the buzzer scream and the indicator rattle. It ran so far under the branches I was sure the carp would get out and walk and I had to keep the rod tip underwater before heading this fish out into the pool.

I remember realising that I was shaking as I played the fish, dreading a similar end to my two previous encounters but the jinx *was* broken and it all seemed so easy again as a dark and broad-backed leather with a huge tail drifted silently over the net; but the action for the morning was not yet over. I had just weighed the leather at two ounces less than the large mirror and the other rod was away, the handle spinning, the rod finally leaving its rests, landing in the mud and slowly moving out into the water! I leapt towards the rod just managing to grab the butt. Up to my knees in mud, with more mud spraying off the reel and covering my face, I felt this was one carp I was sure to lose, but on that morning I probably could have swung it to hand and it wouldn't have dropped off. The Gods were smiling, another fifteen pounder.

But it was to be my last fish from Towertree for some time. The long hot summer was coming to an end and the carp had decided enough was enough. By the time I fished there again a cold wet snap had changed their habits and put them down. I fished several times with nothing further to show for my efforts and finally left Towertree reluctantly for less impressive scenery, the pool once again tranquil and aloof.

Chapter Twenty Five

FURTHER EXPERIENCES AT TOWERTREE

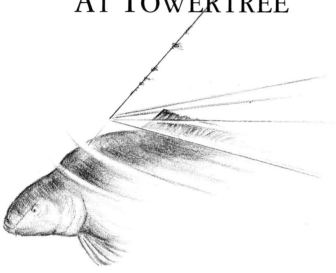

I thought I had learnt much at Towertree during that first summer there. Some carp caught, a successful bait, a successful rig and some definite feeding areas found. So it was with great confidence that I arranged a first trip to Towertree the following summer. The pool was soon to bring me back to earth.

Blank followed blank and I made classic mistakes in my selection of baits. I started there with a new bait for the water, tiny cubes of luncheon meat, but after total failure with this, even with fish over the baited areas, I reverted to the successful particle of last season. The classic mistake in view of the fact that my final visits during the previous year had all been blanks with this bait.

I retraced my tracks; worms, maggots, even corn until the penny dropped.

A *new* particle would do the trick and I began baiting on each subsequent trip. It was difficult, the lake could not be baited regularly due to the infrequency of the trips but I decided to give it a try anyway and was rewarded handsomely on the first trip using the new bait.

It was the first of August; calm, muggy, very still and a bank of mist totally obscured the opposite side of the pool as it became light enough to see.

I cast out both rods just before 4.30am having baited very lightly around the hookbaits with only thirty free offerings. 5am a splash and one bleep on the right hand buzzer indicated a line bite and a fish around that bait, possibly feeding.

Five minutes passed, I had just picked up my notebook and the line to that same rod slowly began to move away. The fish ran all over the show, slack-lined me at least twice and I finally had to wade out to net it more or less on the first try.

The fish didn't seem to know where to go. It seemed confused but it was too late to worry now anyway. As I secured it, the rod pinged straight, the line parting immediately above the trace swivel and I quickly checked that the carp *was* in the net. It was. A good sized mirror with a reddy-orange patch on its tail. 20lbs 8ozs, a fish caught on the first cast with a new bait.

Strange, but I had felt confident about the new bait the previous evening and it had proved correct. Twitches continued to both rods. The fish were still there and I chanced a few more freebies, catapulted individually at long intervals so as not to spook any remaining carp.

No further action and so, just after 6am, I began to rig a camera on the tripod to take some quick shots of the twenty before its return.

"Beeeep!" the left hand rod this time, shaking in its rests. It had been cast almost 90yds to a different area I had baited and cast to as an experiment.

Picking up the rod quickly, I hit into nothing and just kept reeling and reeling. The fish had ran in towards me and to the right, causing a huge bow in the line that had picked up weed and it was only this that I could feel as I regained the line as fast as I could.

Eventually the spool filled and I finally felt the fish that had now ran a considerable distance from where it had first picked up the bait. It dashed this way and that, even more confused than the last fish and I waded out again to net weed and fish as it thrashed wildly.

I bit off the trace this time and carried the fish up the bank to weigh a beautiful, two-tone mirror at 24lbs 9ozs. Two twenties in a session to first and second casts with the new bait. It seemed I was on to something.

Other twenties and doubles followed that season until the bait lost its effectiveness. The next season, the third, I would make no classic mistakes, starting immediately with a

A two-tone mirror; 24lbs 9ozs.

189

new bait but now it was the pool and its carp that were to prove unpredictable and difficult.

It seemed everything I had learnt over the previous two seasons I might as well forget. It was probably down to the weather I supposed. The first two seasons had been hot and still during most sessions. The carp had been much in evidence, giving their presence away constantly and making location a very easy matter by bow-waving, topping, crashing and bubbling. There seemed to be carp everywhere in the warm, shallow water.

This new season, the third, was in total contrast. Global warming and a promise of long hot summers for evermore, had now gone completely out of the window. The constant rain had raised the lake's water level, muddied and cooled the water and reduced the carp to a morbid torpidity.

The lake seemed almost devoid of any carp at all. All their normal haunts within easy range were completely ignored and my lines remained totally still, with even another new bait to tempt them.

It was back to square one. The carp would have to be found all over again, in an area where they would feed and I could reach them.

After scanning the lake intently with binoculars during the first blank session, I had located a small area that seemed to be frequented by carp. There were no definite signs such as leaping or bubbling, just an occassional surface 'humping' that I thought might be carp.

With difficulty, I managed to bait this area and the next session, decided to put all my eggs in one basket and cast both baits there; quite a considerable distance in the torrential downpour that had developed, but it worked - 21lbs 3ozs!

Confidence returning, the new bait successful and I looked forward to some hectic sport, but it was not to be. The next session resulted in a blank and my optimism soon evaporated. Perhaps I had caught the only carp frequenting the new area. I just didn't know what to expect with the next session at the pool, and what did transpire was totally unexpected.

"Beep, beep, beep, beep!" In my dreams, the buzzer indicated the run I had always waited for. That elusive monster had finally chosen one of my baits and I savoured the moment. In reality it was my watch alarm that had shattered the dream and reduced the leviathan once again into fantasy.

Around the house, nothing stirs, not even the cat. So quiet and still, everyone soundly asleep. How it will all change in only a few short hours.

I'm late again, but only by minutes today and following a super-human effort, out of bed, clothes on and down the stairs. Into a drowsy automatic pilot, kettle on, bait from fridge, lunch packed, fill flask, boots ready.

Outside, all is still and quiet, the air cool, but it is not completely dark. The sky looks overcast; no real chance of a hot day to bring the carp out of their hidy-holes. Half asleep still, the journey is hardly remembered save for the fox in the headlights on Sandy Lane but as the car enters the estate, now fully awake, I'm thinking about baiting and swims and casts and wondering what adventures this session might bring.

Through the trees the lake looks still. Mist slides across in regimented columns but only insects and ducks move the glassy surface. No welcoming crash of carp this morning.

Creeping to the waters edge, I fired out some bait into all the usual spots including my new found 'hotspot' that had soon cooled it seemed. The particles hit the water like heavy rain and I hoped the carp had not been alarmed by this weighty downpour.

A small group of deer crashed through the undergrowth behind me, unaware of my presence, but I'd already given the carp a clue and cast out both rods as quietly and quickly as possible, settling down to blend in with the lake and the stillness of dawn, as the sky lightened slowly over the horizon behind me.

After twenty minutes or so, the left hand buzzer uttered a few short, sharp bleeps and fell silent. No ducks or coots over the baited area, I put the action down to a liner; a very good sign. Some fish were over the bait and possibly feeding, I hoped.

Around 5am, intermittant gusts began to ruffle the surface out towards the centre of the pool, shooting strangely in all directions, the wind, like a hooked carp, not knowing which way to go. The gusts soon died away, the lake returning to its usual early morning calm.

"Beep - beep - beeeeeeep! The buzzer interrupted my daydreams. It was 5.40am and I was away on the right hand rod and picked it up as it arched over, a hugh swirl and a deafening splash crashing over the baited area. I thought briefly that it must be a duck, the fish soon correcting my assumption by ploughing of to the left before about-turning and heading for the open water and the centre of the pool.

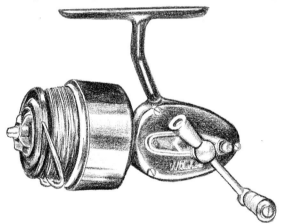

Staying there for quite some time, it headed slowly and purposefully this way and that, the fish finally making up its mind with another about turn and making a beeline for the bank and its snags once again. I side-strained madly, to no avail, as it continued to kite. Under the branches now,

I expected all to go solid at any moment but amazingly it didn't and I pumped and pumped to bring the fish closer and away from danger.

All that remained now was to bring the carp slowly past the six legs of the old boathouse that lay immediately to my left, between me and the fish. As gently as possible, so as not to alarm the fish into flight, I eased the weight passed the first leg; no problem. Then the second; again no problem and approaching the third, but she was away again dashing off back between the first and second legs and beneath the boathouse, a sharp right hand turn and out for the branches once again leaving the line to make horrible grating noises against the wood.

Then all was still. The carp had reached the branches and lay quiet beneath them as I tried not to panic and sort out the situation. Wading out, I passed the rod awkwardly around each leg of the boathouse in turn, trying to maintain some sort of pressure, but it was very difficult, the rod tip pinging off the balcony above me.

Eventually, I passed the rod around the final leg and was once again connected to the carp that I could see clearly laying very close to the branches, docile and still now. It seemed as if all the fight had gone out of her as, very obligingly, she let me ease her forwards and then over the net cord. I lifted and breathed a sigh of relief. It looked a very good fish, perhaps even 25lbs plus, but I was in for a surprise.

As I reached the bank and attempted to lift the net, it came grudgingly and I thought it must be snagged. A closer look revealed the true bulk of the fish and it took a concerted effort to hoist it up the embankment for the weighing ceremony.

The scales zeroed, into a wet sling and I counted as the dial revolved; 10-20-25-26-27-28-29-30! The needle continued to spin, finally resting at 31lbs 4ozs. I subtracted the weight of the wet sling at 9ozs and recorded the impressive mirror at 30lbs 11ozs. A real turn-up for the books. A Norfolk thirty and from a 'wild' water where the fish had grown from fingerlings; not stocked at huge weights as some carp waters nowadays where the carp fishing resembles the pursuit of tame trout.

I returned the fish close to the legs of the boathouse that had caused so many problems and watched as it drifted back into the lake until lost beneath the surface glare, it disappeared from view to become yet another beautiful memory from Towertree Pool.

I returned the fish close to the legs of the boathouse that had caused so many problems.

Chapter Twenty Six

THE GREATEST CHALLENGE OF ALL

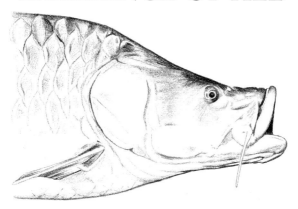

From the top of the hill, we followed the sparkling green river as it cut its way through the arid, dusty and parched landscape of southern India, bringing a brief and relatively narrow margin of almost lush green vegetation to the earth, along with an attendant richness of wildlife of every conceivable nature.

The green band follows bends and straights, often broken by a multitude of stark, grey-black rocks and white foaming rapids that eventually fade into wider, unbroken areas that are the deeper, slower pools.

In these pools and amongst the incredibly ferocious rapids, live the mighty Barbus Tor Mussulah; The gigantic, hump-backed and deep bodied mahseer found only in southern India. The most impressive freshwater fish to be found anywhere in the world and to the freshwater angler, possibly the greatest challenge of all.

For many years I had harboured a dream to travel to India and pursue this legend. Paul Boote had fueled the fire with his original mahseer articles in *Angling* magazine during the late 70's and it is to him that the mahseer anglers of today are totally indebted. Almost single handedly, he

195

opened up the fishing for this remarkable species in both north and south India after certain 'authorities' had claimed that the mahseer was extinct in some rivers!

Having now travelled and fished in India, it is clear what a mammoth and daunting task he must have faced, being the first true mahseer angler since the days of the Raj, without the organised camps that exist today.

And so, from a brief discussion with Dave Plummer in his tackle shop during the close season of 1990, our trip evolved. We discussed the travelling angler and worldwide fishing. I mentioned to Dave that I had no real burning desire to fish for continental carp. There was only one true dream for me and that was to catch a mahseer. Dave's reply was pure gold.

"Let's do it then!"

Names and contacts filed away years previously were hunted out and followed up. Finally, we had whittled our options down to three and after much debate, we booked our camp dates with the most favourable. But in January 1991, it seemed that a Gulf war would stand in our way. Twenty three countries were listed by the Foreign Office as possibly hostile to westerners. Luckily, India was not amongst them although we did hear of Britons being returned prematurely from India prior to our visit.

Our flight, on Air India, was re-routed over Russia but apart from this and an even higher security operation at airports, which we welcomed, the Gulf war had little impact on our trip. Being up-rated to executive class with the help of Nigel Botherway and Air India certainly made for a comfortable and very enjoyable flight.

Once in India, Dave and I were joined by John Bailey and Joy Hurst. John had already caught the northern Indian mahseer (Barbus Tor Putitora) but was keen to pit his skills against the larger variety of the south.

The strange sights, sounds and scents of India are indescribable and must be experienced to be appreciated. Everything seems to get by in a state of disorganised chaos

and India's roads are hair-raising to say the least. How more people are not killed or injured is a miracle in itself. How the taxis and rickshaws manage to negotiate the tiny spaces in between other traffic is a mystery and the use of the horn at all times is obligatory!

From the city, through the suburbs and then into the countryside, the scenery changes dramatically although everywhere during the dry season is hot and dusty.

The cars, motorbikes and rickshaws decreased in number as we entered the countryside, to be replaced by ox carts and lorries painted brightly in colourful designs. Our journey to the river took three hours and even during the midday sun, the miles seemed to flash by with so much to observe, to take in and digest.

After a brief stop to purchase camp supplies, chickens, bananas, coconuts and watched by a spellbound crowd with huge smiles and inquisitive faces we continued on our way.

The road gradually decreased in width and quality until it deteriorated into a dusty, rock and scrub-strewn track as we began to decend through the valley and approach the river.

In the four-wheel drive army truck, we negotiated the dry stream beds and rocky outcrops, hanging on as the truck bounced and juddered, almost toppling over at one point.

Elephant signs were everywhere we looked. Bushes and trees torn and smashed and cannon-ball sized droppings here and there along the track. After a hot and very dusty, but most adventurous journey we began to glimpse the river through the trees and finally the campsite; an idyllic oasis in the unending scrub jungle, and canopied by huge Mutti trees. An ex-army parachute formed a picturesque awning over the central dining area, the tents skirting the perimeter. In between, the ground was regularly swept to keep it reasonably clear of creepy-crawlies. (Unfortunatly, not all uninvited guests were so easily deterred).

Over the days that followed and passed so quickly, we began to catch mahseer . With the help of our expert guides Bola and Suban, we fished hard at dawn and dusk, the midday period usually too hot to endure for long. John was unfortunate to lose the first fish hooked. Estimated at 50-60lbs by the guides, this mahseer simple smashed his rod to pieces.

Under strict guidance at first, from guides that never ceased to astound and amaze us, we fished the rapids and pools with Chilwa, (small deadbaits of a variety of species),

Dave subdued a 40 pounder.

Ragi paste, (a boiled mixture of Millet flour, wheat compound and additives) and spoons.

Our first mahseer landed was, to me, a revelation. A 'green' mahseer with a turquoise hue, as smooth as glass, its huge fins bristling with power even though it weighed a mere 13lbs.

Other mahseer followed as our dreams became reality. Smaller fish from the rapids, followed by 30 and 40 pounders from the deeper pools, John landing several to 44lbs, mostly 'goldens'.

The reliable 'Ragi' seemed to be most productive although lures had their day. John captured a '60' after an epic battle that required him and Suban to follow the fish over one hundred yards downstream in the swirling maelstrom of the rapids, sometimes only the tip of his rod above the water, until they reached the next slow pool where men and fish could regain their composure and the fight could be resumed, and battle won after a truely hard fought fight.

The most productive lure day I missed due to a bout of 'flu' or an Indian equivalent. Dave, John and Joy, accompanied as always by Bola and Suban, had walked upstream in the sweltering midday sun but were justly rewarded for their efforts as a succession of mahseer hit their lures. Some fish were small, some takes missed and with encouragement from John, Joy did extremely well to land a 32 pounder. John had already beaten a 23 earlier and after yet another epic battle in the rapids Dave subdued a 40 pounder, a mahseer to be proud of on the lure.

If the fishing was wonderful, the scenery and wildlife were just as impressive, leaving a myriad of sights and scenes forever imprinted on the memory.

Panther tracks seemed to be everywhere, on both sides of the river. We found them quite close to camp, along the track that led to 'Panther Track Pool'. It was an area of the river we only seemed to fish in the evenings and the walk of perhaps a mile and a half back to the camp in the still darkness on several occasions is one I shall not easily forget.

The feeling of being watched seemed very strong and I was thankful for our guides, one leading and one bringing up the rear. It was akin to a scene from a Jim Corbett book and my admiration for such men was never greater. It takes a very special man of total courage to sit out all night in the Indian jungle waiting for the largest carnivore on earth in the sure knowledge that he is a maneater and is somewhere in the immediate vicinity.

Just after dawn one morning, whilst fishing from the rocks in midstream, the sawing rasp of a panther's roar impressed us for quite some time and seemed uncomfortable close. That night, as we settled down to sleep, the same roar was repeated. An eerie experience in the darkness of the Indian night, with rustlings in the undergrowth and only a canvas tent between you, the scrub jungle and all its inhabitants.

Later that night I awoke with a start. That sound again; now very loud and seeming uncomfortably close. In fact, right outside our tent! I called to Dave; no reply.

I reached for my torch, by now fully awake, and as Dave roused from a heavy sleep, the sound stopped. So had his snoring!

Monkeys, the staple diet of panthers, were everywhere around the campsite and waged constant guerilla warefare on our food supplies, stealing anything left unattended but especially bread and bananas. The brave leader of the pack even managed to enter our tent at one point and rummaged through clothing and bags. We wondered if he and a friend could possibly have made it to Heathrow Airport with our passports and money.

Crocodiles, jackals, hyenas, vultures, eagle owls, fish eagles, kites, four types of kingfisher and a multitude of other birds; scorpions, lizards and large beetles visited our tents and spiders and snakes were seen close to camp. But the only real danger, insisted our guides, would be from elephants, especially lone males or females with young. We were keen not to find out, then one night towards the end of our stay, the elephants came to us!

Late that afternoon, we had heard the first sounds of trumpeting in the distance. When I awoke around 3am, the sounds of elephant were all around and very close. Sounds of branches breaking, of heavy bodies moving in the darkness, of occasional trumpeting and the slow shuffle and thunder of many huge and heavy feet.

"Sssh! Sssh! No torch! No torch!"

The guides seemed more concerned than at any time during our stay as the herd of around fifteen animals slowly filed by. It was impossible to see even moving shadows in the pitch black of night but they seemed almost close enough to touch.

In the morning after breakfast we followed the dinner-plate size prints in the dust of the track until they disappeared into the vastness of the scrub jungle.

Each day that passed seemed magical, with its own special adventures and wonderful sightings but for me, one day outshone them all and will be with me forever.

As usual, the two watch alarms shattered our dreams almost simultaneously. By the time we had shaken out our boots and clothing, (even though they had been hung up) and struggled into our clothes, Anwar was at the tent flap with our tea. Certainly not the best cup of 'Rosy Lea' in the world but hot and wet and a very welcome awakener.

Water bottles filled and tackle assembled, we made our way to the coracles. Down the slight incline in the dim light of the pre-dawn, the black river sliding by silently and invitingly as the jungle slowly came to life.

By the time we had loaded and set off, the sky above the eastern hills had lightened considerably and another beautiful clear, though chilly Indian dawn was upon us.

Bola pulled hard on the paddle in a tight figure of eight at the front of the coracle as he headed the clumbersome craft into the flow, towards the rocks in midstream.

We beached it as silently as we could and Dave and I cast our first baits out at 6.45am, in amongst the 'Crocodile rocks', the big Ragi baits making deafening splashes in the still of the dawn and sat back to await the mahseer with mixed feelings of anticipation and on occassion, unadulterated fear. (I have felt the cold, tight, empty feeling in the pit of my stomach as a mahseer take occurs and can only describe it as enjoyable terror!)

We three sat in silence listening to the sounds of the dawn.

"Did you do it?" Did you do it?" repeated the red wattled lapwing as pied kingfishers flashed by and brahminy kites wheeled overhead and as the great white-gold disc slowly peeped over the hills, flooding the valley with new light, large splashes far downstream reflected in its rays and betrayed the presence of striking crocodiles.

After only an hour in this swim with no sign of action, we boarded the coracle once again and drifted silently downstream on the flow to a new swim below Crocodile Rocks, passing a family of six inquisitive otters on the way.

We pulled the coracle onto the bank and cast our baits

into the central flow, feeling the lines until they found the bottom.

We had fished the swim on previous occasions and felt its special aura before. Whether it was the depth of the river here or its width or the rock formations and trees, or a combination of all these factors, we knew this swim was special and held the possiblity and promise of a big fish.

And we were not to be disappointed.

After less than half an hour, I had recast my bait and shortly afterwards, the ratchet on the 7000c began to scream like never before as line rapidly emptied from the spool. Literally shocked into action and shaking with surprise and fear I tried vainly to slow down this exodus, setting my thumb on fire in the process. I quickly knocked the reel into gear, the rod doubling over but the exodus continued, the reel now screaching in short, sharp bursts.

"Zizz - zizz - zizz - zizz!"

"Coracle Sir! Coracle quick! Big fish! Big fish!"

Bola had recognised the situation in an instant as the reel continued to empty and I jumped aboard in a daze and sat down, pushing the rod butt between my legs and pumping hard to regain some of the lost line.

I had cast perhaps 30 yards, the fish running off well over 100 yards, possibly even 120 yards, which meant only around 30 yards left of the 40 pound line. And still it ran.

Unseen, irresistible power pulled us slowly into midstream and I found it impossible to exert real pressure. The mahseer was simply towing us! Drifting and dragged, we followed the fish downstream and gradually the spool began to fill again and look more healthy

Still in midstream, we had now cut down the distance between fish and coracle, regaining line all the time, Bola battling with the paddle to keep pressure on this irresistible force. Then suddenly, this pressure on the rod relaxed.

"I think its off!" I cried to Bola in despair, but disappointment was brief. The huge fish had either found

the rocks momentarily or my line had flicked off a scale or fin.

The rod wrenched over once again, the mahseer heading uncontrollably for the left hand bank. We had no choice; we followed. It veered right again into the midstream flow now very deep and very slow.

"Bank Sir! Bank!" Bola headed the coracle towards this bank and I realised his logic. On such a fish, we had no leverage whilst afloat. It just towed us where it wanted us.

He dragged the coracle into a small inlet and I leapt out onto dry land, now feeling more in control but the fight was far from over.

204

Although less erratic now, the battle raged on and I realised for the first time the wisdom of the rod harness I had left back at camp. Every seering run, meant sharp pain and I was forced to crouch, pushing the rod butt into the sand to exert real leverage. At least I had regained most of the line. I remembered the old cliché, 'and then the bottom moved' and suddenly it seemed totally relevant.

A concentrated effort in towards my own downstream bank required heavy sidestrain to head the fish back into the flow not knowing if unseen roots and snags lay hidden at the edge.

After half an hour we gained our first glimpse, a gigantic flash of criss-crossed gold deep beneath the surface and then she was gone again, only to return more clearly after yet another powerful, screaming loss of line.

The first real sight of that mahseer on the surface in the early morning was simply quite staggering. It was more whale than fish and as I walked slowly backwards, she kited to the right and I reeled hard, the leviathan heading into a small inlet, burying its nose in a reedbed in a final flurry of water and spray as Bola pounced upon her, threading the stringer through and securing one of the greastest of all angling prizes, a mahseer of over one hundred pounds.

When secure, Bola's arm disappeared inside the cavenous mouth as he extracted the huge 6/0 hook. It took only an instant.

"Hook out. Very lightly hooked!" he casually informed me!

Bola and I towed her slowly back across the river, he paddling the coracle and I with the stringer wrapped very securely around my hand with visions of being dragged over the side at any moment. Dave awaited patiently on the rocks with scales and cameras; the crocodiles immediately downstream had prevented him from following us to film the fight closely from his bank.

Bola's initial estimate had been 90 pounds. Now, as he cradled the fish and tied on an extra stringer he raised his estimate.

"Over 100 pounds!" he said confidently with a huge grin and a twinkle in his eye.

The scales proved him correct. 104 pounds of gigantic, hump-backed, 'golden' mahseer. What a beautiful and awe inspiring creature.

Somehow, the news travelled like lightening, even through the scrub jungle and a crowd, including John, Joy, Suban and Johnny Jensen (who was later to take an incredible 92 pounder) had soon assembled from our camp with a battery of cameras, smiles and congratulations.

Water flooded off the fish as I lifted, the assembled crowd silent now, a kaleidoscope of thoughts forever imprinting on the memory.

The feel of those huge golden scales, edged with gun-metal blue; the enormous, fleshy, sail-like fins shot with pinks and blues; the white barbels, inches long; the swivelling, all-knowing eye and the sheer effort required to lift such a monstous fish after an exhausting battle; finally reduced to celluloid and memories as she glided through my arms past Bola, dorsal and tail fins moving the surface and then was gone as if it had all been a dream. I doubted that such an adventure would ever really sink into my conciousness to become just another everyday reality.

"Give us a smile Steve!" demanded J.B. for a last fishless photograph.

It wasn't difficult. I just kept shaking my head in disbelief, the number 'one-o-four' ringing inside it.

"I'll wake up... tomorrow", I replied in a daze.

Chapter Twenty Seven

A LINE ON THE WATER

The beauty spot and its steep embankment had changed little in over thirty years. The river had been less fortunate. The fair-haired man, accompanied by three children, walked cautiously down the steep incline to the reed-fringed river that lay below. They emerged from the canopy of the beech trees into the warmth of the sun and headed towards the first bend, along the overgrown path, the children reminded that now was the time to be silent.

The river was much slower than in years gone by, the weed growth less luxuriant. The lack of flow had allowed a build-up of 'scum-weed' to cover sand and gravel patches of the riverbed and impede the growth of the once prolific streamer weed. Minnows and 'pin-heads' were still present in great numbers and deeper in the clear water, amongst the swaying forest of weed, slightly larger fish could occasionally be seen darting and flashing as they fought the minnows for their share of the white grubs.

The red tipped float carrying the maggots once again moved slowly downstream on the flow. Young eyes sparkled as the float disappeared once again, this time without preliminary bobs and dips. A larger quarry had beaten the minnows to the bait and a line on the water began to move, the tip of the old rod curving over once again...

207